"A masterful overview of pivotal changes in the global economy by one of the world's leading experts on logistics and supply chains." **Julian Jessop, Independent Economist**

"This book helps re-examine the decisions and drivers around globalization at different time and place and helps establish a foundation for re-assessment and re-engagement. A must read for any global thinker." **John Rendon, President of the Rendon Group, a Global Strategic Engagement Consultancy**

"For decades, trade grew faster than the economy, expenditures on inventory holding declined, and the average distance travelled per ton of seaborne cargo went up. Then came covid, trade wars, and the energy transition. Does this mean the end of globalization?" **Jan Hoffmann Head, Trade Logistics Branch, UNCTAD**

"John Manners-Bell's book is top notch. In the West we need to wake up to the stark fact that the Old Order has shifted. China has all the capabilities available to become the premier Global Power and the ramifications of its incursions into Africa and the Indian Ocean Rim, for example, have largely gone unnoticed. We need to be very worried." **Malcolm Warr OBE, Chair, Critical National Infrastructure, Scotland**

"Building upon his deep knowledge and extensive practical experience, the author highlights how political forces, more than economics, are now shaping supply chain structures. Clearly written, forcefully argued, the book vividly illustrates how such forces, combined with ethics and environmental considerations, are driving the profound structural changes we can witness today." **Anne Miroux, Faculty Fellow at the Emerging Markets Institute, Johnson School of Management at Cornell University**

"John Manners-Bell's latest book The Death of Globalization captures the very essence of current board room discussions around the world. This book explores all the key dynamics influencing re-shoring, near-shoring and friend-shoring decisions – and sets the scene for a gradual de-globalisation trend, with the world moving towards regional supply chains. Essential reading for every business executive and the entire supply chain and logistics fraternity." **Mark Millar, Keynote Speaker, Trusted Advisor, and Author of Global Supply Chain Ecosystems**

"John eloquently argues about the multifaceted influence of economic, political and environmental pressures on modern supply chains. Critically, the book highlights the importance of ethics affecting how stakeholders across the value chain make decisions that shape the (de)globalised world we live in." **Dr Vaggelis Giannikas, Associate Professor, School of Management, University of Bath**

THE DEATH OF
GLOBALIZATION

THE DEATH OF GLOBALIZATION

How Politics, Ethics and the Environment
Are Transforming Global Supply Chains

John Manners-Bell

Published by Sea Pen Books 2023

Sea Pen Books Ltd
18 Northburn Avenue
Rubislaw
Aberdeen
Aberdeenshire
Scotland
United Kingdom
AB15 6AH

www.seapenbooks.com

A CIP catalogue record for this book is available from the British Library

ISBN 9781739350802

Printed and bound by CPI Group (UK) Ltd, Croydon, CR0 4YY

Typeset by Deanta, 8 The Seapoint Building, 44-45 Clontarf Road, Clontarf, Dublin 3, Ireland

Contents

Figures and tables

FIGURES

TABLES

Preface

It wasn't meant to be this way. China's accession to the World Trade Organization was supposed to herald a new era of open markets and free trade allowing Western companies access to China's large and increasingly prosperous population whilst integrating the country into the global trading regime. This singular, globalized market would naturally be led by the world's most powerful economy, the USA, which would also be the main beneficiary.

Whilst the benefits of globalization have indeed been transformative for the world's economy (although not unalloyed as I will go on to discuss), politically and economically it was China, not the USA, which gained the most. However, instead of growing closer to the West in terms of culture and democratic values as many in the US and Europe had naively hoped, China's government used its newly gained economic influence to project political power into Asia, Africa, Latin America and even Europe, challenging the post-war world order. In many ways Western policy towards China in the 2000s was an earlier version of Germany's more recent 'Wandel durch Handel' ('Change through trade') approach to Russia. In both cases, the belief that exposure to Western business practices, social and political freedoms and increasing prosperity would result in the adoption of liberal democracy and free markets has proved ill-conceived.

Instead, China has developed a 'market socialist' alternative in which political and commercial interests have become intertwined. Nowhere is this more apparent than in the new

Chinese multinational 'challengers', such as high-tech manufacturer Huawei, which many Western intelligence agencies
believe to be an extension of the state apparatus. Governments
are only recently waking up to the risks to energy, communications, financial and technology infrastructure which these
companies may represent.

Increasing geopolitical tensions, not least Russia's invasion of Ukraine and China's threat to Taiwan, have led many
governments and companies to re-evaluate the security of the
globalized ecosystems which underpin international trade and
economic development. As a result, new supply chain hegemonies are developing based on the concept of 'ally' or 'friend
shoring' rather than economic rationale. An extension of this
policy is the ambition of 'strategic autonomy': governments in
the West and China are determined to reduce their dependence
on potentially hostile countries for critical products and raw
materials. The practicality of this policy is yet to be seen, especially when it involves critically scarce minerals or the development of enormously expensive manufacturing capabilities,
such as semiconductor fabrication plants. At the very least,
however, such moves will provide significant headwinds to the
growth of international trade in strategically important sectors.

Whilst Chinese economic ascendancy and its newly developed political influence has caused Western governments to
question many of the tenets of globalization, domestic politics have also played a role in undermining accepted supply
chain doctrine. Offshoring production has resulted in 'collat-
eral damage' to parts of society, especially those communities
formerly dependent on employment in heavy industry. The
development of the resulting so-called 'rust belt' areas has
been exploited by populist politicians who claim to represent
those ignored by governments, media interests, big business
and intergovernmental organizations over which normal people have little or no control – the so-called 'democratic deficit'. The election of President Trump in the US has been the
most obvious example of a politician coming to power with an

anti-globalization mandate, resulting in free trade agreements being ripped up and a trade war with China (and to a lesser extent the EU and UK).

Whilst it would be tempting to apportion responsibility for the fragmentation of world trade to President Trump. Protectionist measures including tariffs and non-tariff barriers have been increasing in the United States since the Great Recession of 2008 and even after the Trump administration President Biden has maintained many of the trade barriers previously erected. In fact, Biden's latest Inflation Reduction Act (IRA) has gone way beyond the previous administration in terms of subsidizing parts of the US economy. Making subsidy contingent on the production of goods in the US – necessarily at the expense of its trade partners – has caused significant anger even amongst its closest allies in Europe. What is clear is that protectionism and subvention, discredited by the majority of economists and politicians only a few years previously, have now been revived, rehabilitated and readopted into mainstream political orthodoxy throughout the West. 'Industrial policy' – the idea that governments should select and support specific sectors – is back in fashion, despite evidence that such an approach is hugely costly and counter-productive (Panagariya, 2019).

The imposition of tariffs by consecutive administrations on Chinese (and European) goods may not have benefited the US economy – one estimate suggests that they have resulted in the loss of 173,000 jobs (York, 2022) – but they have brought about significant changes in supply chain strategies and global trading patterns. Not least, they have driven the growth of 'China plus' alternative markets such as Vietnam and Thailand which have benefited from the diversification of manufacturing locations away from China. Many global manufacturers are now adopting far more nuanced supply chain strategies integrating various remote suppliers ('far-shoring') with those based closer to home markets ('near-sourcing') or even repatriating production completely ('reshoring'). This is also partly due to the mitigation of other risks such as the concentration of production in areas prone to natural disasters and the vulnerability of international transportation to bottlenecks such as the Suez Canal or capacity issues within the West Coast ports of the USA. However, political measures are arguably the most important factor in the transformation of supply chain structures.

That being said, globalization is not just under pressure from geopolitics or domestic pressures. It has also faced criticism from environmental campaigners highlighting the carbon-intensive nature of the transportation of components and products around the world. Ethical considerations also need to be taken into account regarding the conditions of workers at remote, offshored suppliers or those involved in mining virgin materials destined for use in consumer goods or 'green' technologies.

The aim of this book is to highlight the political, ethical and environmental forces which are driving structural and deep-rooted change, challenging the orthodoxy of globalization. It is clear that the market landscape will become hypercomplex and difficult to navigate, making the decisions made by both politicians and supply chain leaders ever more critical. A global recession, the resurgence of nationalism, fears for the environment, the Covid-19 crisis and growing geo-political tensions have resulted in the re-emergence of trade barriers amidst toxic international relations. Neo-protectionism has transformed the economic landscape and supply chains are now being shaped by political rather than commercial imperatives. Fragmented, localized, fractured...globalization, if not completely dead, is on life support.

REFERENCES

Panagariya, A (2019) Debunking Protectionist Myths: Free Trade, the Developing World, and Prosperity, Cato Institute. Available from www.cato.org/economic-development- bulletin/debunking -protectionist-myths-free-trade-developing-world-prosperity

York, E (2022) Tracking the Economic Impact of US Tariffs and Retaliatory Actions, Tax Foundation. Available from https:// taxfoundation.org/tariffs-trump-trade-war/

1

A Framework for Understanding Deglobalization

INTRODUCTION

Decades of liberalization of international trade relations, including the removal of many tariffs and non-tariff barriers, have enabled global supply chains to develop on the basis of economic rather than political imperatives. This is no longer the case. Following the Great Recession of 2008/9, politicians in both emerging and Western markets began to challenge the mantra of globalization due, not least, to perceptions of its effect on workers; damage to the environment; inequitable flows of finance; heightened risk and its role in facilitating China's economic and military rise. This meant that even before the systemic disruption of supply chains caused by the Covid-19 pandemic, governments right across the political spectrum had already started to adopt protectionist policies whilst promoting subsidy-driven national industrial strategies.

This chapter summarizes the reasons why global supply chains are undergoing a transformation and the role that politics will play in shaping the supply chain structures of the future.

GROWING RISK IN SUPPLY CHAINS

For decades, globalization has remained unchallenged as the pre-eminent political and economic orthodoxy. A shift change in transport cost structure (largely resulting from the advent of containerized shipping in the 1950s), the liberalization of trade regimes, advances in information and communications technology (ICT) and the opening up of low-cost labour markets (predominantly China), drove a transformation of production strategies. Manufacturing processes have been 'unbundled' and outsourced on a global basis, creating virtual networks connected by worldwide data, financial and logistics systems.

As with all characterizations, however, this only tells part of the story. The major short-term wins which resulted from both lower labour costs and access to new and increasingly lucrative global markets, blinded management to longer-term systemic risks.

Supply chains became vulnerable to a whole range of threats which were either little understood or ignored. The difficulties in costing these risks – especially disruption caused by high-impact, low-probability events – led managers to focus on the reduction of more easily quantifiable costs – such as labour and inventory.

A number of unrelated events in the period following the Great Recession of 2008/9 demonstrated the weakness of this approach. In the first instance, economic shockwaves resulting from a downturn in consumer demand led many manufacturers to cancel orders from their Asia-based suppliers forcing many into bankruptcy. When the economy picked back up again, manufacturers found that they were unable to meet demand leading to considerable economic damage lasting much longer than the recession itself.

This was shortly followed by two major natural disasters: the Tohoku earthquake and tsunami of 2011, which disrupted many Japanese electronics, chemicals and automotive suppliers and halted production at factories across Asia, North America and Europe; and the Thai floods of the same year which affected a cluster of critical hard-disk drive manufacturers and had a similar impact on the global high-tech sector. Both these events exposed the lack of visibility which manufacturers had into their upstream suppliers, the interdependence of production networks and the risks involved in single/sole sourcing of components.

Furthermore, in 2013 the textile and clothing sector was rocked by a factory collapse in Bangladesh which killed over a thousand workers. This revealed to a global audience the poor conditions and pay of many workers employed by Asian-based suppliers of Western manufacturers and resulted in considerable damage to the equity of many international brands. This was reinforced subsequently by a number of scandals related to suppliers' poor environmental practices, especially in China; the 'modern slavery' endemic in parts of the world and revelations about illegal mining of conflict minerals – many of which are used in consumer electronics – taking place in war-ravaged Congo.

Whilst the impact of these events on their own may have been short-lived, together they created a growing awareness at boardroom level that supply chain risk could have existential implications. At the same time, the consequences of the failure of critical supply chains started to become apparent to Western politicians, although, as we will see, it wasn't until the Covid-19 crisis that the full risks of offshoring production were exposed.

THE WORLD WAS NEVER 'FLAT'

Trade has always been a source of political contention, not least in the post-war period. With the fall of Communism in the 1980s; the success of the General Agreement on Tariffs and Trade (GATT), the predecessor of the World Trade Organization (WTO); and closer integration in Europe, North America and Asia, it seemed to many that the model of Western democracy and economic liberalism would become universal. This resulted in such books as Francis Fukuyama's *The End of History and the Last Man* and Thomas Friedman's *The World is Flat*, two titles which characterized the belief that systems which embraced political and economic freedoms were the

Figure 1.1 Changing political priorities.

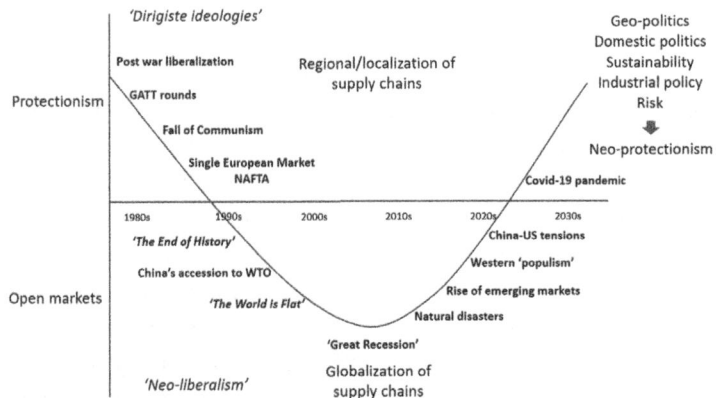

Source: Author.

culmination of humanity's socio-economic evolution. Both books captured the zeitgeist of the period before the Great Recession, even accounting for the 9/11 terrorist attack on the World Trade Center.

This optimism was seemingly reinforced by China's accession to the WTO in 2001. At the time many people believed that integrating China into global supply chains, taking many millions out of poverty and providing Chinese consumers with a 'taste' of the West would ultimately bring about political change. Whilst the Communist Party talked about creating a 'socialist market economy with Chinese characteristics', this was considered by Western politicians as a step on the inevitable pathway to free market economics and democracy. The West's thinking can best be summed up by the German phrase, 'Wandel durch Handel' – 'Change through trade' – although, as has been seen, this was wildly optimistic.

Rather, China used the wealth and know-how it gained from integration with global supply chains to promote its own economic – and subsequently political – agenda. Not content with a role as 'Asia's assembly plant', undertaking low-value, labour-intensive manufacturing activities, Chinese companies were encouraged by the government to achieve global leadership, often through acquisition (e.g. Lenovo's purchase of IBM's PC business in 2005). Since then, China's policy has been to focus on capturing increased levels of supply chain value by producing high-tech components which had previously been the preserve of companies based in countries such as Japan or Korea. In effect, the Chinese government's industrial policy has led to the consolidation of upstream manufacturing processes within its own border as opposed to participation in 'factory Asia' networks – the previously dominant virtual manufacturing model underpinned by cross-border, just-in-time (JIT) movements of intermediate goods throughout the region.

The vast wealth which China has amassed along the way has provided it with the political and military resources to extend its influence throughout much of the emerging world and even into Europe, not least through its 'Belt and Road Initiative' (BRI). However, the benefits of globalization have not only accrued to China. As we will see, other emerging markets such as Turkey and Saudi Arabia have developed their own distinct economic and political systems which have to a greater or lesser extent eschewed Western neo-liberalism, challenging global and regional hegemonies.

Whilst it is fair to say that the relationship between many emerging markets and the West has always been characterized by a certain level of mistrust, the Great Recession confirmed these doubts in many peoples' minds. As investment from banks in Europe and North America dried up, governments looked to China to fill the void and confidence in the neo-liberal paradigm was shaken further. Such doubts have only been re-affirmed by the Covid-19 pandemic when China once again won the plaudits for its 'vaccine diplomacy' (being the first to supply countries within its sphere of influence with doses of Covid-19 vaccine) and its willingness to supply shipments of personal protective equipment (PPE). This appeared to contrast with Western governments' hoarding of vaccine doses and imposition of export bans on critical medical supplies. Although this was not a wholly true characterization of the situation and the effectiveness of the Chinese vaccine was unclear, it certainly fuelled the perception throughout much of the developing world that trade rules could be ripped up when it suited powerful governments. This has caused possibly irreparable damage to the West's position on promoting open markets and free trade.

CHALLENGES TO GLOBALIZATION

This book will examine the economic, political, security and sustainability challenges which globalization presently faces. Some of these challenges could be described as headwinds, reducing growth in intercontinental trade flows and promoting a return to localized, or at least regionalized, supply chains. Others, such as the 'de-Sinofication' of advanced technology sectors (such as semiconductor manufacturing) represent a transformation of supply chain thinking and structures. What is clear is that political factors have become far more influential in the development of supply chains and this has combined with a re-thinking and re-calculation of the economic benefits to create a much more nuanced and complex business environment.

As Figure 1.2 shows, the majority of challenges facing globalization are either policy driven (that is, administrators' desire to reform globalization to create a 'fairer' world – a vision shared both by 'populists' and 'the establishment', albeit from vastly different perspectives. Or the challenges stem indirectly from policy decisions addressing major global issues such as sustainability and international security, including geopolitics. It could be argued that economic challenges are relatively minor in comparison and whilst there is no doubt that on their own they would lead to some level of change (e.g. 'China plus' strategies to mitigate single sourcing risks) they are not enough to drive root and branch transformation. In fact, the market is already developing its own solutions to some of the problems that have been faced in the past decade, such as by

Figure 1.2 Challenges to globalization.

Economic

Sole/single sourcing risks
Infrastructure capacity
Market volatility
Vulnerability to natural disasters
Energy crises
Strikes/blockades
Shipping rates
Currency wars

Policy reform

Lack of democratic accountability
Developing countries left behind
Unfair distribution of wealth
Tax avoidance by multinationals
Tariffs/trade wars
Rust Belts
Cultural homogenization
Immigration

International security

Dependency on foreign governments and imports
Geo-political tensions
China's Belt and Road Initiative
Advanced tech 'bleed' to foreign powers
Dual supply chains
Vulnerability to cyber crime
Terrorism and piracy
Corruption

Sustainability

'Race to bottom' carbon leaking
Global value chain carbon intensity
Shipping/air cargo emissions
Lack of environmental oversight
Responsibility for worker conditions
Climate change adaptation

Source: Author.

increasing supply chain visibility through technological innovation. This could be referred to as 'process innovation' rather than the disruption which political interventions could lead to.

POLICY REFORM: THE RISE OF POPULISM AND PROTECTIONISM

Mistrust of globalization and its mechanisms has become entrenched globally. However, whilst there has always been suspicion of the role played by multinationals in emerging markets, it could be argued that just as damaging has been a loss of faith in the model amongst Western electorates.

Whilst consumers have undoubtedly benefited from lower costs and a better range of products, many parts of Western society have lost out. Millions of manufacturing jobs have been moved from North America and Europe to Asia hollowing out former industrial hubs, such as the 'Rust Belt' in the USA. These areas have provided fertile ground for politicians eager to exploit levels of dissatisfaction with the establishment and this has given rise to populist leaders such as Donald Trump and, arguably, the anti-EU vote in the Brexit referendum.

Much of the damage to US manufacturing occurred in the 2000s following China's accession to the WTO. As alluded to in the last section, the offshoring trend was driven *inter alia* by low labour costs, access to huge workforces and a weak Chinese renminbi. Regarding this latter point, the political ramifications of the Chinese government's aggressive currency policy are well covered in Professor Helen Thompson's book, *Disorder* (Thompson, 2022). In essence, the policy of keeping the renminbi artificially low meant that Chinese manufacturers had a major advantage over their US competitors. Whilst there were protests in Washington, the US government's response was moderated by the fact that many US-owned global corporations, such as Apple and Walmart, were actually benefiting very significantly from the relative strength of the dollar, as were American consumers.

The scale of the impact on US manufacturing, however, cannot be underestimated. In 2001 there were still 17.1 million people employed in this sector. Only three years later this figure had fallen to 14.3 million, dropping further to 11.5 million after the Great Recession (although since then there has been a gradual recovery) (Harris, 2020).

However, the damage was already done. As Thompson comments, '[This destruction] spurred class conflict in American democratic politics: those who gained were shareholders and extremely well-paid executives; those who lost were factory workers'. Both Democrat and Republican parties were held responsible for the loss of such a totemic part of the US economy and society leading to the election of President Trump on an avowedly populist, anti-free trade manifesto. He quickly moved to impose tariffs on imports from China and Europe, withdraw from the Trans-Pacific Partnership and re-negotiate NAFTA.

Nevertheless, it would be wrong to suggest that neo-protectionism started and finished with the Trump administration. According to the Swedish National Board of Trade, the net number of new trade restrictive measures introduced by G20 countries since the recession of 2008 had risen from 300 in 2010 to almost 1100 by 2015 (Kommerskollegium, 2016). Since 2016, the number of discriminatory measures implemented accelerated as populism took root before 'exploding' in 2020 as countries reacted to Covid-19. In that year, there were over 2000 new measures recorded. A similar picture emerges in terms of domestic subsidies. There was a steady increase in the decade after the Great Recession before a threefold rise in 2018 and a further doubling in 2020 (IISD, 2021). Opposition to free trade and globalization is a longer-term and more global phenomenon than just President Trump's administration or Brexit.

GLOBALIZATION STANDS ACCUSED

In a paper entitled 'Taking back control of globalisation', Benoît Cœuré, member of the Executive Board of the European Central Bank, lists four main charges against globalization (Cœuré, 2018).

It creates financial volatility

The global integration of the banking sector triggers and amplifies financial shocks such as the Asian financial crisis of the 1990s, the euro-area sovereign debt crisis and the 'Great Recession' of 2008/9.

There is a lack of 'fairness'

Not all countries abide by the same set of rules leading to accusations of dumping practices, an environmental race to the bottom…or currency manipulation.

It embeds inequality

A global labour market has impacted on employees in developed countries as jobs are offshored. At the same time multinationals and global tech platforms have subverted taxation rules to benefit the richest in society.

It is outside democratic control

The institutions established to oversee the rules of globalization are remote and unaccountable and a 'cosy cabal' exists between multinationals, politicians and lobby organisations, such as the World Economic Forum.

Whilst Cœuré accepts that there is some truth in these charges, his view, which reflects what could be termed as that of 'the establishment', is that many of the criticisms could be addressed by increasing the robustness of the institutions which oversee globalization. He references the way in which the EU has created a market based on fair competition and common standards; implemented a European Stability Mechanism (ESM) to assist members in crisis; its strengthening of financial regulation and supervision; the restoration of fiscal buffers; and its leadership in preventing companies from avoiding tax by profit shifting.

These institutions – the 'bureaucracy' (used in its purest, non-pejorative sense) and judiciary – exist either to implement or to enforce laws enacted by the legislature. They can take either a supervisory or facilitatory role. As regards globalization of trade, the most important inter-governmental organization is the WTO, as already mentioned. Rather than becoming stronger as Cœuré might have hoped, however, the WTO has become a shadow of its former self. Not only has it failed to advance trade liberalization over the past two decades but it has become side-lined by the world's largest trading partners. In short:

- The organization is accused of failing to prevent China abusing the international trade regime.
- Under both Obama and Trump administrations, the US has blocked new appointments to the WTO's appellate body which has prevented its ability to mediate in disputes.

- The EU has established an alternative dispute resolution mechanism, further marginalizing the WTO.

Although support for free trade and open markets has dwindled, governments have successfully cooperated to address many people's concerns over unfair tax avoidance by multinationals, a significant cause of disquiet (see Chapter 3). However, the fact remains that the remoteness of the institutions and political organizations doing deals on behalf of their electorates will continue to raise questions over both their legitimacy and the legitimacy of the entire globalization 'project'.

Ironically, given that it is one of the most mistrusted of these institutions, the World Economic Forum (WEF) has identified that 'new-thinking' is required to provide a more inclusive vision for future global cooperation: one which spreads economic, political, societal, technological and environmental benefits and costs more equitably, using the Covid-19 crisis as a positive catalyst for change. Such terms as 'Build Back Better', the 'Great Reset' and 'responsible capitalism' have been coined to describe the opportunities to enhance and 'improve' the economic system and address many of the perceived problems of globalization.

The WEF's ambition has three main themes (WEF, 2020):

1. Encouraging 'stakeholder capitalism'
2. Combining economic development and sustainability and
3. Leveraging the Fourth Industrial Revolution (4IR).

Businesses, according to WEF, should be dedicated to fostering 'values' rather than 'value creation', an aspiration endorsed by, amongst others, the International Monetary Fund, the General Secretary of the United Nations, the president of the European Central Bank and the president of the EU Commission. Outside of these institutions it would be fair to say that the idea hasn't been wholly well received, with criticism emanating from all sides of the political debate. One 'free market' review of the vision suggests that it, '...is based on a fundamental lack of appreciation of the power of markets to bring about desirable social outcomes. In calling for a break with the traditional capitalist model, it leads to a world in which pressing social, environmental, and political challenges are exacerbated rather than alleviated' (Foss et al, 2022).

From a political perspective, other critics are more visceral in their opinions. They believe that the 'Great Reset' is either utopian and unachievable or is designed to consolidate the power of the 'metropolitan elite' and the various undemocratic institutions which are already held responsible for the deleterious impact which globalization has had upon Western and emerging market societies.

RESHORING AND INDUSTRIAL POLICIES

As we demonstrate in Chapter 10, many governments have needed no second invitation to support businesses or erect barriers to protect manufacturing and retailing markets. These invariably are very popular with the electorate even though in the long term they are often counterproductive. Making the case for open markets is certainly more difficult than slogan-driven policies which involve, for example, 'taking action to protect jobs' as it requires an understanding of the benefits of a liberalized trade policy plus an ideological commitment. Both have been lacking over the past decade especially with a vacuum of leadership from the WTO which has become mired in unsuccessful trade negotiations.

For a whole host of reasons, not least cultural, the creation of manufacturing jobs has become a major political imperative. Although this does not strictly require government subsidy, in reality this is often the case. There can be economic, strategic or security imperatives behind attracting manufacturing jobs back from Asia (reshoring), as I go on to discuss. However, in many other cases, the reasons are often nakedly political and the results disastrous – governments are very bad at backing 'winners' and often capricious with tax spend due to competing priorities.

Many countries have adopted support policies for 'infant-industries', that is, those which, in the opinion of politicians, might go on to thrive but have been let down by a market failure, lack of foresight or capital. In some cases, this support might take the form of financial subsidy. In others, the government may play a facilitatory role in creating the environment or 'eco-system' in which new businesses can develop, such as clusters of suppliers, training or ICT networks. In the past, high levels of investment have been shown to successfully kickstart an industry such as semiconductor manufacturing in Japan in the 1970s or ship building in China in the 2000s, by 'engineering comparative advantage' (The Economist, 2023). However, history is littered with evidence of examples of when industrial strategy has failed, not least the British government's support for electric vehicle battery manufacturer, British Volt. Not only is subsidy expensive and often futile, but it can disadvantage consumers by keeping prices artificially high. It can also tie up capital and actually reduce innovation by artificially extending the life of companies with failed business models or technologies.

CHINA'S INFLUENCE ON GLOBALIZAITON...AND DEGLOBALIZATION

China's role in globalization in the 2000s cannot be overstated – and nor can its role in de-globalization. This is due partly to its own changing domestic political and economic priorities as well as the response to its development from the rest of the world.

Increasing domestic focus

Whilst China's government has made public pronouncements on the importance of globalization, this runs counter, to some extent, to its desire to capture as much supply chain value as it can from its trade partners. According to the OECD, 70 percent of international trade is destined for production in global value chains (GVCs), that is, supply chains in which intermediate goods are manufactured in a number of countries before assembly and then exported to the end-user market (OECD, 2022). The OECD believes that fragmentation of production (unbundling and outsourcing) has already peaked as a result of some of the reasons outlined below. However, in the case of China, there has been a specific and concerted policy effort to develop advanced manufacturing capabilities which will allow Chinese OEMs to replace foreign suppliers. This has resulted in a significant reduction of what the OECD calls 'backward linkages' as more input components of final products are made domestically.

Illustrating this trend (Figure 1.3), in 2005 over a quarter of exports from China relating to global value chains contained foreign content. By 2015 this had fallen to about 17 percent (ECB, 2022).

On top of this, the imposition under President Trump of US trade tariffs on Chinese imports has resulted in an 'In China, for China' industrial strategy. Encouraged by the country's political leaders, consumers are purchasing Chinese-made rather

Figure 1.3 Foreign value add of exports from global value chains – China.

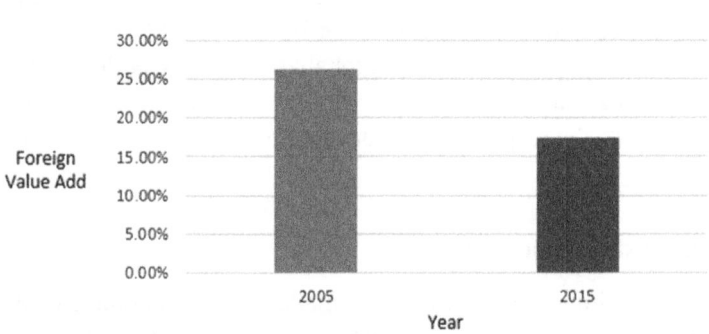

Source: OECD (2022).

than foreign products in increasing volumes, a significant shift in behaviour from only a few years ago. This trend is particularly evident in the younger demographic which takes pride in buying domestically produced goods. These trends will result in China becoming more self-sufficient in both intermediate goods as well as finished products. In other words, entire supply chains, 'from cradle to grave', will remain within China's borders.

Fracturing international relations

The last decade has witnessed the development of a fissure between the West and China in terms of international relations. Globalization has successfully contributed to China's advance as many in the West had originally hoped. However, what was not envisaged was the direction the Chinese government would take, exploiting its position of strength as the world's largest manufacturer to push forward its own assertive political agenda, extending its 'soft power' throughout the world and directly challenging neighbours in the Asia-Pacific region. A military invasion of Taiwan is now being regarded as a possibility – if not a probability – by many strategists in the West, which would obviously have economic as well as political ramifications, given Taiwan's dominant position in semiconductor chip supply chains.

There have also been growing concerns that Western technologies have been put to use in a military context by Chinese companies which are acting under the direction of the Chinese government. In summary:

- Western security agencies are concerned about potential cyber vulnerabilities which remotely manufactured electronics could possess, either due to malign forces or simply lack of quality control. One example of this is the role of Huawei in the development of 5G infrastructure which is dealt with in Chapter 5.

- Western governments would like to deny 'adversaries' (mainly China but also Russia, North Korea, Syria and Iran) the defence capabilities which advanced technologies (such as types of semiconductor) can provide. This is discussed in Chapter 6.

From a security perspective, many politicians believe that reshoring as much production of sensitive material as possible would help to address both of these concerns as it would make all the processes more transparent and the companies involved answerable to Western oversight. This would also address the risk of exported technologies 'bleeding' from commercial to military use.

But there are counter-arguments to this view which question the extent of the threat posed by countries such as China. It has been estimated that 92 percent of the value of the semiconductor supply chain is already generated by the US and its allies (Wei, 2022) whilst China accounts for just 6 percent. SMIC, China's largest fabricator, can only produce 45 nm chips, two generations behind the most advanced manufacturers. Indeed, Taiwan's semiconductor industry has been described as a 'silicon-shield' against China, that is, the industry has become so essential to the global and Chinese economy that China could not afford to risk destroying it through an invasion across the straits. China may also consider that the more integrated Taiwan's chip industry is within US supply chains, the more likely the US would be to defend the island against Chinese aggression. In fact, plans in the West to build its downstream chip manufacturing capabilities will only weaken the 'shield' and make an invasion more, rather than less, likely.

Expanding the 'Sinosphere'

Over the last few years China has invested more than one trillion dollars in infrastructure projects building links to countries in Asia, Africa, Latin America and the Middle East, the so-called Belt and Road Initiative (BRI). By offering finance at very cheap rates it has been able to extend its political influence. The area which the BRI covers is equivalent to 55 percent of global GDP, 70 percent of the global population, and gives it influence in regions where 75 percent of known energy reserves are located (WEF, 2016). As an example of China's growing influence in the emerging world, in Latin America, 19 out of 24 countries have signed up as strategic partners to the initiative, including Mexico.

One of the results of the BRI is the development of Sino-centric supply chains. Raw materials flow into China from resource-rich regions, whilst its finished goods flow back into these markets. In terms of logistics, many international operators find themselves locked out of the contracts to move these goods, with the main beneficiaries being Chinese-based companies.

To counter what they see as a strategic threat – the projection of China's soft power – the US and the EU have plans of their own to finance infrastructure projects in emerging markets, but nowhere near on the same scale.

DOMESTIC GROWTH ECLIPSES TRADE

During the 1990s and for most of the 2000s trade volumes grew at a rate which was roughly double that of GDP. However, from the time of the Great Recession in 2008, the ratio between GDP and trade growth was replaced with one of direct parity: 1:1 or less. In 2019, before the period of intense volatility caused by the pandemic, global GDP growth was 2.5 percent whilst trade volumes had decreased by 0.1 percent.

This changing dynamic had been caused by a number of reasons including:

- Trade tensions and protectionism (most recently demonstrated by the US–China trade war).
- A strengthening of the Chinese currency which had been kept at an artificially low rate through a dollar peg.

- A reduction in import demand due to economic downturn in developed countries.
- A rebalancing of risk from far-sourcing to near-sourcing and reshoring policies.
- Decreasing wage differentials between developed and developing markets.
- Changing investment priorities of countries which have focused on stimulating the domestic economy and infrastructure rather than exports.
- The reduction in one-off gains from offshoring.

Research jointly conducted in June 2022 by market research organization Ti Insight and the Foundation for Future Supply Chain (FFSC), confirmed that globalization is no longer regarded as the pre-eminent economic force it once was. Findings revealed that the overwhelming majority of the senior logistics and supply chain executives in the survey believed that a major transformation of supply chains was already

Figure 1.4 Industry executive opinion on the future of global supply chains.

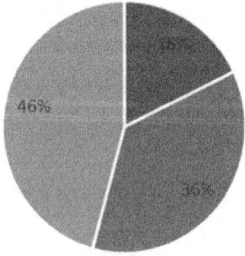

■ Globalization in its present form is here to stay

■ Security tensions between China/Russia and US/Europe will lead to new supply chain hegemonies based on 'ally-sourcing'

■ Supply chains will become substantially more fragmented and localized as a result of protectionism, risk, costs and re-shoring

Source: Ti/Foundation for Future Supply Chain.

Figure 1.5 Inter and intra-regional trade flows 2021.

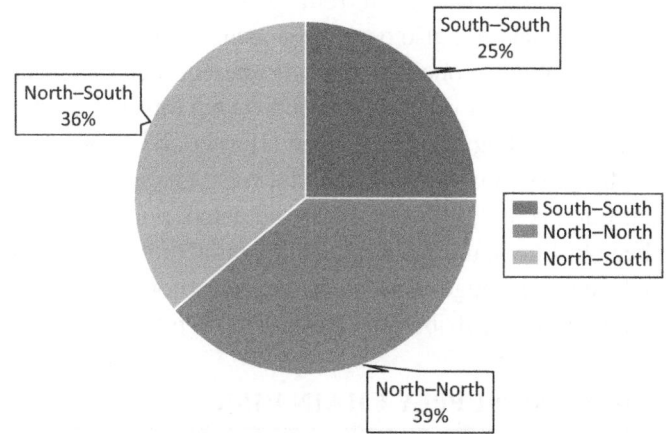

Source: UNCTAD (2022).

under way. Just 18 percent of 129 executives agreed with the statement 'globalization in its present form is here to stay' whilst over a third (36 percent) agreed that 'security tensions between China/Russia and US/Europe will lead to new supply chain hegemonies based on "ally-sourcing". Nearly half (46 percent) thought that 'supply chains will become substantially more fragmented and localized as a result of protectionism, risk, costs and re-shoring'.

From global to regional trade flows

The world's transition from a globalized to a regionalized economy is no more evident than in the growth of 'South–South' trade. This term is used to describe trade which occurs between developing countries including on an Intra-Asian basis as well as between Asia, Africa and Latin America.

In 2021, South–South trade was valued at $5.4 trillion. To put things in perspective, it has been estimated that South–South trade accounted for just 12.8 percent of all trade in 2000. By

2022, this proportion had almost doubled to 25 percent whereas North–North trade had fallen from about half of global trade to 39 percent. There has also been a change in the profile of goods moved. As Asian economies have prospered, there has been a growing demand for not just intermediate but finished goods, as consumer spending power has risen (Horner and Navdi, 2018). The 'Made in China, consumed in the West' characterization of global trade is looking increasingly outdated, a fact which has not been lost upon the multinational manufacturers which have already invested huge sums in local production facilities and national/regional distribution networks to supply these markets.

MITIGATING SUPPLY CHAIN RISKS

As already mentioned, the threats to globalization stem not only from political sources. Global manufacturers have increasingly come to realize that many of the costs relating to global supply chains have been 'hidden' or, at least, ignored. Single sourcing strategies have been shown up as unsustainable in a world which is characterized by volatility, uncertainty, complexity and ambiguity (VUCA). This approach has been likened to a householder refusing to pay for insurance on the balance of probability that their house won't burn down. Whilst it will save money in the short term, in the longer term it could prove catastrophic.

In a supply chain context, even if there are a number of years without a natural disaster, geo-political conflict or economic crisis, a 'reversion to the mean' is inevitable. Those businesses which don't have the agility or flexibility to react or rebound from such events will be at best put at a competitive disadvantage, at worst face an existential crisis. Therefore, even without political intervention encouraging or forcing manufacturers to diversify their supplier base to a number of markets, it is likely that manufacturers would have done so anyway albeit at a slower rate.

Of course, this doesn't mean the end to global flows of goods. What it does mean is that sourcing strategies will become more nuanced. For example, a Western manufacturer may decide to keep its main Chinese supplier but add a layer of redundancy to their supplier base by developing a partnership with a Vietnamese company (so-called *'China plus'*) as well as looking to reshore or near-source. This is best described as the migration from a 'unipolar' to a 'multipolar' world (Chapter 9).

This is not the cheapest approach in terms of production, inventory management and transportation but it is 'safer'. Having said that, all routes from Asia were disrupted by the West Coast ports congestion of 2021/2. Shipping, port, rail and trucking infrastructure was overwhelmed by the surge in spending which resulted from the US government's Covid-19 stimulus package. This has given weight to the reshoring argument and in a broader context the development of industrial policies (Chapter 10).

ENERGY PRESSURES ON THE WEST

As is discussed in more detail in Chapter 7, the world is certainly not 'flat' in terms of energy resources. This seemingly self-evident point has huge significance in terms of industry's access to cheap oil, gas and coal supplies, a fact which has been brutally reinforced to European governments, businesses and consumers in the aftermath of the Russian invasion of Ukraine.

Germany's economy, focused on energy-intensive manufacturing, has been amongst the worst affected. At the height of the crisis, gas input costs soared to multiple times those of US competitors making many German businesses uncompetitive on the world market. Whilst the US can rely on domestic supplies and therefore is largely immune to the global forces impacting much of the rest of the world, many large European users of gas, such as fertilizer manufacturers, have already been forced to shut down production, creating shortages and price increases.

Although the US and China enjoy cheaper energy costs than Europe, one of the biggest regions to benefit will be the Middle East. Countries such as Saudi Arabia are investing heavily in making their countries compatible with Western business needs – better transport and ICT infrastructure, for example. This, combined with the advantage of consistent supplies of cheap oil and gas (as well as renewables), will result in the region becoming a much bigger manufacturing hub for energy-intensive industries.

TECHNOLOGY

Technological innovations have had a pronounced 'flattening' effect on supply chains. They have allowed managers, wherever in the world they may be, to have real-time visibility of production schedules, shipment status, estimated delivery times and a whole host of other information wherever their products are being manufactured. This has mitigated many of the risks involved in offshoring to remote, low-cost labour markets. For example, supply chain risk management software is now able to alert managers to congestion, bad weather, industrial action and many other threats, allowing re-routing decisions to be made or for goods to be sourced from alternative suppliers.

One of the consequences and benefits of this level of visibility is that inventory has been 'replaced' by data. Retailers and manufacturers have been able to reduce levels of 'buffer' or 'safety' stock held in case of lost or delayed shipments as management can exert more operational control driven by data availability. Eventually advances in technology will mean that logistics and supply chain decisions will be made hyper-efficiently by artificial intelligence. Of course, technology is not a panacea. During the trans-Pacific shipping crisis caused by the Covid-19 pandemic, technology played a limited role in ameliorating the impact of congestion at West Coast ports. The systemic failure of physical transport infrastructure could not be overcome by any digital innovation, although in the long term digitization and automation will undoubtedly increase efficiencies, capacity and throughput.

However, just as physical supply chains look likely to fragment, so too will digital flows of data. The likelihood is that there will be a further decoupling of the US and Europe from China in terms of data and technology due to concerns over privacy and security. This is discussed in Chapter 13.

Cyber attacks are another risk to global supply chain data, a threat posed by criminal or state actors. There are multiple examples of disruption to the logistics industry – shipping lines and express parcels providers have fallen victim to instances of so-called 'ransomware' costing companies billions of dollars. The risk will only escalate as corporations become almost totally reliant on technology. As Jim Hagemann Snabe, chairman of A.P. Møller-Mærsk, commented at the time of a major cyber attack on his company in 2017, it will not be possible to overcome such events in the future by 'human resilience' alone (Manners-Bell, 2020).

Automation could also play a major role in de-globalization. By lessening the importance of labour costs to the outsourcing process, many manufacturers may find that it is more cost-efficient to produce goods closer to the end market, rather than offshore. Government policy (including tax policy) may well promote such investment as a way of increasing productivity. However, this is not the only potential outcome. Automation could also lead to greater levels of wealth inequality as corporations and other owners of capital benefit from the value which is created rather than employees. One government response to this would be to strengthen the power of labour organizations and workers, subsequently increasing wage pressures, or raise taxes on corporations which would then delay productivity increases.

CONCLUSION

The development of global supply chains had already started to run out of steam following the Great Recession of 2008. Offshoring of production had slowed, not least as a result of narrowing wage differentials and the fact that a large proportion of Western manufacturing had already migrated to Asia in the 1990s and 2000s. At about the same time, corporations started to realize that outsourcing production to remote locations was not risk-free – they had just ignored threats such as natural disasters and reputational costs related to the environmental and societal impacts of their supply chain decisions. However, the real transformation has been brought about by a change in political landscape, accelerated by the Covid-19 crisis. Decades of trade liberalization are being rolled back as governments around the world have become far more interventionist, increasing trade barriers and adopting 'industrial strategies' to support local jobs and businesses. Geopolitical tensions between the US and China (not to mention Russia's invasion of Ukraine) have led to export controls on advanced technology and environmental legislation will result in new carbon border taxes.

The inevitable result of these political measures – each no doubt justifiable in its own right – will be the 'Balkanization' or fragmentation of supply chains. This will not be without consequences. From an economic perspective, supply chains will become sub-optimized, leading to higher inflationary pressures, higher levels of costly inventory and less availability of products. The judgement of whether this is a price worth paying is one largely influenced by political perspective.

REFERENCES

Cœuré, B (2018) Taking back control of globalisation: sovereignty through European integration, European Central Bank. Available from www.ecb.europa.eu/press/inter/date/2018/html/ecb.in180328.en.html

ECB (2022) Global value chains: measurement, trends and drivers, European Central Bank. Available from www.ecb.europa.eu/pub/pdf/scpops/ecb.op289~95a0e7d24f.en.pdf

Economist, The (2023) Warnings from history for a new era of industrial policy, The Economist, January 11 2023.

Foss, N, Klein, P and Murtinu, S (2022) The economy doesn't need a reset, and neither does management theory, Scandinavian Journal of Management. Available from https://doi.org/10.1016/j.scaman.2022.101214

Friedman, T (2007) The World is Flat, Penguin

Fukuyama, F (1993) The End of History and the Last Man, Penguin

Harris, K (2020) Forty years of falling manufacturing employment, Bureau of Labor Statistics. Available from https://www.bls.gov/opub/btn/volume-9/forty-years-of-falling-manufacturing-employment.htm

Horner, R & Navdi, K (2018) Global value chains and the rise of the Global South: unpacking twenty-first century polycentric trade, Wiley. Available from https://onlinelibrary.wiley.com/doi/pdf/10.1111/glob.12180

IISD (2021) Rising Protectionism Signals Valuable Lessons Have Been Forgotten, International Institute for Sustainable Development. Available from www.iisd.org/articles/rising-protectionism-signals-valuable-lessons-forgotten

Kommerskollegium (2016) Protectionism in the 21st Century, National Board of Trade. Available from www.kommerskollegium.se/globalassets/publikationer/rapporter/2016/publ-protectionism-in-the-21st-century.pdf

Manners-Bell, J (2020) Supply Chain Risk Management, Kogan Page, London.

OECD (2022) The trade policy implications of global value chains, OECD. Available from www.oecd.org/trade/topics/global-value-chains-and-trade/

Thompson, H (2022) Disorder, Oxford University Press, UK

UNCTAD (2022) UNCTAD Handbook of Statistics 2022, UNCTAD. Available from https://unctad.org/system/files/official-document/tdstat47_FS02_en.pdf

Wei, C (2022) Are Semiconductors a National Security Issue? The Diplomat. Available from https://thediplomat.com/2022/04/are-semiconductors-a-national-security-issue/

WEF (2016) Why China could lead the next phase of globalization, World Economic Forum. Available from www.weforum.org/agenda/2016/11/china-lead-globalization-after-united-states/

WEF (2020) The Great Reset, World Economic Forum. Available from www.weforum.org/great-reset/

2

Political Risk and New Economic Protectionism

INTRODUCTION

As discussed in Chapter 1, globalization has come under attack from both ends of the political spectrum. Many believe it has resulted in a hollowing out of previously industrialized regions, such as the 'Rust Belt' in the USA, as well as damaging the economies and societies of emerging markets, not to mention the environment. For whatever reason, the prevailing antipathy has caused governments, Western or developing, populist, democratic or authoritarian to become far more interventionist than had been the case since the 1970s. This is partly the result of events such as the Great Recession and the Covid-19 pandemic, but it is also a result of the weakening of institutions such as the World Trade Organization (WTO) which for years has flown the flag of open markets.

WEAPONIZING SUPPLY CHAINS

Whilst the structuring of supply chains in the past four decades has been driven by the economic imperative of ensuring product availability, low labour costs, low transport costs and inventory efficiency, the role governments have played in influencing location of production and supply chain structures has been largely ignored.

That this is the case is the result of the unsung success of trade liberalization. The World Trade Organization played a fundamental role in 'flattening the world', reducing trade barriers to such an extent that, from a business process perspective, it became as easy and cost-effective for manufacturers to source or produce goods in a remote country as in their home market. With these process issues sorted out, companies could focus on the operational challenges.

Of course, in reality, government intervention in supply chains has never gone away. Although it would seem obvious that countries have an interest in stimulating economic growth by encouraging direct investment from foreign manufacturers and banks, many politicians wish to balance this aim with protecting local markets. This has resulted in a complex and often contradictory policy framework implemented by governments that, to use a term coined by former UK Prime Minister, Boris Johnson, want to 'have their cake and eat it' (or 'cakeism' as it subsequently became known). That is, countries want to:

1. encourage foreign investment which brings with it jobs and know-how
2. place as many barriers in the way of foreign imports as possible
3. ensure unfettered access to international markets for their own exporters.

China, unsurprisingly, has been the most successful proponent of 'cakeism' or as it is officially termed, the 'Bringing in, Going out' policy. Membership of the WTO in 2002 was a crucial part of this agenda. As academics, Christensen and Hearson write, 'WTO membership has enabled inward and outward integration of firms into global value chains, yet has been marked by both highly selective negotiation, implementation and enforcement across corporate sectors and policy areas, depending on the domestic political and economic context'. In other words, China uses WTO rules when it suits its purposes or as the authors euphemistically put it, 'China engages in new ways with global rules and norms...seeking to support, protect and enable its economic ascension' (Christensen and Hearson, 2022). In a paper for international affairs think tank, Chatham House, authors Horton and Hopewell put it more bluntly. 'China lacks credibility as a defender of the rules-based trading system because of its own use of protectionist trade policies, and its attempts to weaponize trade as an instrument of economic coercion' (Horton and Hopewell, 2021).

However, China has not been alone in this policy. As will be discussed, all countries are to a greater or lesser degree guilty of such behaviour, including developed markets such as the US. Former president Trump has been accused of undermining the WTO through his actions (see below) and despite the view that as the former vice president to Barack Obama, President Biden, '...appreciated the value of diplomacy and the power of multilateral institutions' (Cebeci, 2020), his actions have not matched this aspiration. As a policy adviser for the Cato Institute puts it:

The Biden administration's trade policy...seems increasingly to be merely a smoother and more polished version of the same turning away from the wider world, of the same myopic mercantilist view of how the United States should address trade domestically, and of how it should engage in trade and trade relations globally. So far, US trade policy in the Biden administration has been the reign of polite protectionism.

(Bacchus, 2022)

As part of the restoration of America's position within international institutions, a return to a functioning relationship with the World Trade Organization was expected. However, this clearly has not happened as discussed below (*Retrenchment in the USA*).

This chapter will look at the new wave of protectionism which has taken root across the world and the complicated system of trade barriers, incentives and taxation policies which are influencing supply chain architecture.

PROTECTIONISM V2.0

The EU's strategic autonomy

The EU characterizes itself as being on a journey towards what it calls 'strategic autonomy' or 'strategic sovereignty', that is, the capacity to act in strategically important policy areas without dependence or recourse to other countries. Efforts towards this goal have been given impetus by various events occurring in what it calls a 'hostile geopolitical environment' (EPRS, 2022). These include, according to the EU at any rate, Brexit, the election of President Trump and the increasing importance of China on the world stage. The onset of the Covid-19 pandemic led the EU to urgently review its economic resilience, followed of course by the ramifications of Russia's invasion of Ukraine, especially in terms of energy policy.

That being said, there is little consensus amongst EU partners on what the idea of strategic autonomy should mean for the EU in terms of industrial and trade policy. Whilst Germany's policy of embracing globalization reflects the fact that its economy is highly dependent on trade with China, France has been keener on a more mercantilist approach predicated on the goal of building and protecting 'national heroes'. This has led to tensions between Europe's largest economies, laid bare when President Macron's demand to join a visit organized by Chancellor Scholz to meet President Xi Jinping in China in 2022 was rebuffed.

Although European policy seems to have been influenced to a large degree by France's 'dirigiste' agenda, there has been pushback from countries in addition to Germany. In 2021, The Netherlands and Spain published a joint 'non-paper' (European-speak for a paper put forward for discussion in a closed session without attribution), promoting the concept of 'open strategic autonomy'. In it the authors stated that, 'Rather than independence, what strategic autonomy must foster is greater resilience and interdependence, in the context of more balanced, and better governed globalization, in which interoperability must prevail over uniformity'. It went on to say, 'At the same time, the EU must uphold its commitment to open economies and societies. The EU's strategic autonomy does not imply isolationism or economic protectionism; rather it should be built on principles of multilateralism, cooperation and rules-based free trade, without undermining the interests of the least developed countries'.

It is unsurprising that Spain and The Netherlands have sought a commitment from the European Commission to its founding principles of free markets. Both countries fear that their own businesses could lose out if larger neighbours start to subsidize their 'national heroes'. The Netherlands' economy is also particularly exposed to international trade and any barriers which the EU may erect will disproportionately impact its ports and airports.

Although the EU believes that it needs to attain increased levels of independence and self-determination in the face of an assertive China and in light of lessons learnt from the Covid-19 crisis and Russia's invasion of Ukraine, there is still disagreement on how and if this can be achieved. There is an innate tension stemming from China's conflicting role as a customer, supplier and competitor, both economically and, increasingly, from a security perspective.

China, on the other hand, sees Europe's growing animosity and the rule-setting influence it believes it can project through its economic scale as an attempt to rebuild Western power in emerging markets which was lost in the post-colonial era. Although this theme may suit its own political purposes, there is no doubt that it also has considerable traction amongst other countries in the emerging world.

An uneasy and complex relationship with China is not the only headache for the European Commission. It also faces a US administration which is willing to spend vast sums of money to stimulate its own economy, with seemingly little concern for the repercussions which its policies may have on its trade partners, 'friendly' or not. The consequence of Biden's aggressive package of Inflation Reduction Act (IRA) subsidies, many of which are likely to breach WTO covenants, has been to encourage calls for a similar 'Buy European' Act. As France's president Macron said, 'Europe cannot be the only place in the world that doesn't have a Buy European Act and the only place in the world where you still have a state aid system that sets rules as if there was no external competition' (*Financial Times*, 2022).

The sense of disquiet over the future of European industry in the face of a sustained challenge by competing nations ignoring or exploiting the present international trade regime has been exacerbated by the energy crisis. Not only are manufacturers being 'pulled' away from producing goods or investing in Europe by attractive incentives, but they are also being 'pushed' by high energy costs. If there is a new wave of offshoring, this may well precipitate 'buy European' legislation, creating in effect a global subsidy arms race.

Retrenchment in the USA

Although a chasm divides many of the policies of the Trump and Biden administrations, both have largely been united in their approach to supporting, subsidizing and protecting the US economy. Under Trump, the USA followed a policy of retrenchment, both economically and militarily, under the banner 'America First'. This included the initiation of a trade war with China which continues to this day.

President Trump took the view that international trade is what could be termed a 'nil sum' game. In other words, he believed that, rather than a process in which value accrues to all parties, trade is a contest in which there are winners and losers. Moreover, prior to his administration, he believed that the US had been losing, especially to China (but also to Europe and immediate neighbours, Mexico and Canada). This state of affairs, in his mind at least, was largely due to the weakness of the WTO which had failed to address China's unfair trade practices. Trump believed that this failure provided him with the justification to sideline and ignore the WTO's dispute resolution mechanism (although it should be noted that President Obama had started this process years earlier by blocking the appointment of judges to the appellate body) and he embarked on a trade war with China, imposed tariffs on other trade partners such as the EU and UK and violated the rules of the WTO through unilateral trade actions (Horton and Hopewell, 2021).

Has there been a change of approach since the election of President Biden? Certainly, since his election President Biden has continued what he sees as the prioritization of US manufacturing and jobs by passing legislation which he believes strengthens domestic supply chains as well as national security. This includes passing the 'Build America Buy America' Act, part of the Infrastructure Investment and Jobs Act of November 2021, which according to the official US government website, www.madeinamerica.gov, is designed to 'reduce the need to spend taxpayer dollars on foreign-made goods'.

He also introduced the 'Build Back Better' plan, which after opposition in the Senate, morphed into the 'Inflation Reduction Act' of 2022. It is estimated that the act will raise $739 billion through the introduction of 15 percent corporate minimum taxation rate, reform of drug pricing and tax enforcement. These revenues are to be spent on energy security and climate change, affordable care and deficit reduction (n.b. the law, named as such to sell it to the public, will have a negligible effect on reducing inflation in the short term).

Despite its seemingly innocuous title, the act has attracted opprobrium both within and outside the USA. The devil, as far as foreign observers are concerned, is in the detail of the act's provisions. For example, electric vehicles made by large automotive manufacturers will become eligible for tax credits now a cap on volumes has been removed. The credit, worth $7,500, will stimulate electric vehicle (EV) sales helping the US to meet its carbon emissions targets. However, in order to qualify, the final assembly of these EVs must take place in the US. In addition, batteries will be required to have at least 50 percent North American content, rising to 100 percent in 2028, and mineral content from China and other 'foreign entities of concern' (e.g., Russia) will need to be reduced to 20 percent by 2026, replaced instead by materials sourced from 'free trade' partners.

Whilst these regulations may have been aimed at China, the fact that the EU and UK do not have free trade agreements in place means that they are similarly affected. Every EV manufactured by companies such as GM and Tesla will in effect receive a subsidy of $7,500, which will, of course, severely damage the sales of their European competitors. The IRA will also include provisions for a 30 percent tax credit on the cost of new or upgraded plants manufacturing renewable energy components.

The EU is particularly worried about what it sees as discrimination and is considering taking the US to arbitration under WTO rules if discussions cannot resolve the issues. 'We are in talks with the Americans so we do not start a kind of trade war now', German Economy Minister Robert Habeck is reported as saying (Alkousaa, 2022). The fear is that European manufacturers will move substantial parts of their production and supply chain to the USA. There is also a belief that future exemption of European manufacturers might be a bargaining chip in negotiations over the implementation of the EU's Carbon Border Adjustment Mechanism (CBAM), which will apply to trade with countries which do not already levy a tax on carbon emissions, a measure causing disquiet in Washington (see Chapter 11).

'Protect in India'?

The 'Make in India' initiative was established in 2014 by Prime Minister Narendra Modi as a way of encouraging investment in advanced manufacturing as well as fostering innovation and skill development. An important part of the policy includes the improvement of transport and information and communications technology infrastructure and the creation of production eco-systems which will subsequently attract global manufacturers. The aim was to propel double-digit economic growth, create 100 million additional manufacturing jobs and increase manufacturing's share of the economy to 25 percent by 2022 (a target now pushed back to 2025).

As such, the programme resembles many others introduced throughout the developed and emerging world. However, alongside promoting investment initiatives, 'Make in India' has also been accompanied by a raft of measures aimed at protecting companies from imports of consumer goods, electronics and textiles. In large part, goods emanating from China have been targeted.

Whilst the policy was designed to reduce dependence on foreign markets, the result has been protectionism, hurting consumers and reinforcing inefficiencies. One commentator dubbed the initiative as 'Protect in India' rather than 'Make in India' (Swaminathan, 2018a). What's more, critics have pointed out that the proliferation of new tariffs on imports has encouraged the misdeclaration of goods (in order to benefit from lower tariff rates) in collaboration with corrupt customs officials as well as cronyism as sectors and businesses lobby for special treatment (Swaminathan, 2018).

The stance of the Indian government towards trade policy is complicated by internal politics. On one hand, there are those that fear the impact which the entry of multinational corporations into the Indian market would have on small businesses, in particular retailers. Regulations have consequently constrained the ambitions of international retailers such as Walmart and e-commerce players such as Amazon. On the other, there are those who believe that China provides the greater threat, dumping cheap, subsidized exports on the Indian market to destabilize the economy and support its political goals of expansionism. It is worth noting that Modi has ensured that India is one of the few countries in the Asian region to oppose China's Belt and Road Initiative, unlike its major rival and neighbour, Pakistan.

Historically, the result of post-independence protectionist policies has been that India, to a large degree, has excluded itself from the world's economy. The intent of 'Make in India' was to achieve the opposite, that is, a closer integration with global value chains. However, the way that Modi has gone about this could be described as counter-intuitive. He believes that by raising duties by up to 25 percent on many imported intermediate products, he can encourage global suppliers to establish Indian operations and hence increase domestic value add. The so-called 'phased manufacturing programme' (PMP) started raising duties on specific components used in mobile phones in 2016 and rapidly expanded this list in subsequent years. The original ambition of the PMP was to ensure that up to 50 percent of the value of a mobile phone assembled in India was generated by Indian-based suppliers (rather than imports), thereby establishing an ecosystem for foreign investment and allowing Indian high-tech companies to participate in global value chains (Aulakh, 2017).

A policy that purports to support the aims of globalization by implementing a system of higher duties, tariffs and non-tariff barriers obviously sends a mixed message to the outside world. Likewise, attempting to differentiate between Western multi-nationals and Chinese corporations is also problematic, both practically and politically. There is a significant risk for the Indian economy that even though trade barriers may be erected to support the engagement of a nascent sector with a global value chain, the result may be a slide back to the days of full-scale protectionism and subvention, undoing years of reform.

Happily for Modi, his plans may gain a boost from geo-political and economic forces. As manufacturers diversify their supplier base and production locations out of China, they are looking for new sourcing options. As is evident from the Apple case study in Chapter 9, 'Make in India' has at the very least facilitated the development of an ecosystem which can tempt global manufacturers either to set up or expand operations in the country. However, the risk is as the world approaches a period of sustained economic downturn that an archaic protectionist regime will isolate India further from globalized supply chains rather than lead to its closer integration.

AMAZON RETREATS AGAIN FROM INDIA

Global e-tailing platform, Amazon, announced in November 2022 that it was intending to discontinue its 'Amazon Distribution' business which serves retail customers in Bengaluru, Mysore and Hubli with e-commerce wholesaling services. The service was largely aimed at *kiranas,* neighbourhood nanostores based in urban areas.

Part of Amazon's problems in the market come from well-resourced local competitors, such as Reliance Retail, Meesho and DealShare. However, the government has also put many barriers in its way including legislation which bans foreign retailers from holding inventory. This means that multinational retailers can only do business in India if they do so through stakes in local companies. Proposed legislation may even remove this loophole.

This is part of Prime Minister Modi's push to make India more self-reliant. As well as preventing foreign investment in the market, he has imposed a tax on digital services which has also hurt global platforms. This policy has been enthusiastically embraced by Mukesh Ambani, the chairman of Reliance Industries and a supporter of Modi. He is quoted as saying, 'We have to collectively launch a new movement against data colonization. For India to succeed in this data-driven revolution, we will have to migrate the control and ownership of Indian data back to India – in other words, Indian wealth back to every Indian' (Singh, 2021).

When Modi came to power in 2014 he promised market liberalization and welcomed investment from foreign companies. It was hoped that his election would precipitate a new era for India, engaging more closely with international value chains and integrating more closely with the global economy. This seems an increasingly remote prospect.

Made in China 2025

As already discussed, China stands accused of using the global trade regime to penetrate foreign markets whilst ensuring that large parts of its economy remain protected from external competition. At the centre of complaints is the government's Made in China (MIC) 2025 policy which aims to propel China's high-tech sector to a world-leading position helped by a combination of:

- subsidies
- market access restrictions placed on foreign companies
- the acquisition of intellectual property through forced joint ventures in China's domestic market
- the acquisition of intellectual property through foreign acquisitions
- government investment funds
- local government support
- government-led domestic market consolidation (to create 'champions') and
- the 'mobilising' of state-owned enterprises and increasingly state-directed private companies to fulfil the goals of this policy.

The sectors being targeted by the Chinese government for support include:

- electric vehicles
- robotics
- aerospace equipment
- modern railway equipment
- wind turbines and green energy technologies
- biologics.

In fact, the entire programme, developed in 2015 with a ten-year time horizon, is modelled on Germany's equivalent – Industry 4.0. Where the policy differed, and the reason for the criticism, is that it included detailed quotas of the proportion of components and goods that would be manufactured in China by Chinese companies. By 2025, China wants to be 70 percent self-sufficient in high-tech industries and a world leader by 2049.

The programme has explicit aims and sets out the methods which will be employed to enable goals to be met. But it is also alleged that, in addition to the national, publicly stated plans, China also encourages regional governments to pursue clandestine anti-competitive policies, blocking international access to markets whilst supporting local companies. This makes it far more difficult for other countries to prove that China has been breaking its commitments under the WTO agreement.

Direct and indirect support is a very important part of the MIC policy and comes in multiple forms. According to the European Union Chamber of Commerce in China (EUCCC), Chinese companies in the relevant sectors are able to access support from both local and national government in the form of:

- direct subsidy
- waiver of environmental regulations
- loans from state-owned banks on non-commercial terms
- support to customers, covering part of the price of products or cost of installation
- local government procurement strategy.

According to the EUCCC, '...in many cases this support is only made available to companies in which foreigners hold no equity or to companies that make purchases from domestic firms' (EUCCC, 2017). One example given by the European Chamber highlights the difficulties which European rail equipment manufacturers are facing in the country. The technology gap has closed between foreign and local companies due to forced technology transfers as a result of joint ventures and Chinese manufacturers are benefiting from preferential access to the domestic market.

Cyber security regulations are another tool being used by China's government to make it more difficult for foreign companies to supply the Chinese market. Following legislation passed in 2017, all foreign companies must submit their products to security inspection if they are to be used by the Communist Party or government or used in any of the industry sectors covered by the MIC policy. Whilst this has had obvious negative impacts on Western exporters, there will also be consequences for the Chinese economy, with Chinese companies unable to access world-leading technologies due to the policy of enforced local substitution.

One way of getting round this is to gain access to the technology through acquisition of leading Western firms. This is of obvious concern to many governments, fearful that the Chinese government is providing 'shopping lists' for state-owned or directed companies as well as the resources to make the acquisitions. This has led to the EU, UK and US passing legislation allowing M&A authorities to take a view on the security implications of an acquisition by a foreign-owned entity if it is considered of strategic importance.

One such deal was the acquisition of an Italian drone manufacturer, Alpi, by a consortium of companies including Chinese-owned CRRC and a group controlled by Wuxi municipal government. Although the buyers did not notify the Italian authorities as required by regulations, a screening process revealed the links and the 'dual use' nature of the technology being acquired, that is, the opportunities to leverage commercial technology in a military role. Although in this case the potential for sensitive technology to 'bleed' into the hands of the Chinese was identified, the opacity of ownership structures can make it very difficult to screen buyers effectively.

THE US–CHINA TRADE WAR

The US–China trade war has already led to a major impact on global flows of goods over the last four years. Most of the tariffs imposed by the US have targeted the B2B sector (rather than B2C) and hence global value chains have been the most affected. Intermediate products represent 57 percent of the total value of goods which now attract tariffs.

Part of the aim was to encourage reshoring and increase the level of US exports. A study undertaken by the US Department of Commerce suggests that at present US manufacturers import 20 percent of their intermediate goods compared with 15 percent in 1997. The research indicated that if offshoring was rolled back to the levels last seen in 1997 the US would import around $180 billion less product. This would constitute a reduction in Chinese exports of 2.1 percent (White House, 2021).

However, there is little evidence that the tariffs are having a material benefit for the US economy. In fact, there have been a number of negative unintended consequences of the policy. By 2020:

- Exports of goods affected by tariffs on inputs of intermediate components dropped by 2 percent.
- Employment numbers dropped: 300,000 jobs were lost.
- US companies paid $46 billion more in tariffs than they otherwise would have done.
- Tariffs cost the average US household $600 a year.
- There is no evidence that China purchased more US goods – the original aim of the phase one trade deal (Lobosco, 2020).

Although protectionism has not led to benefits for the US economy, it has resulted in geographic diversification of GVCs away from China. This could be regarded as positive indirect result of the trade war by reducing a systemic over-reliance on the market. Consequently, many multinationals have looked at various 'optionalization' strategies which have included reshoring, near-sourcing or 'China plus' (i.e., sourcing goods from China plus one or more alternative countries).

Some of the main beneficiaries of these policies have been low-cost countries (LCCs) in Asia such as Vietnam. According to the US International Trade Commission, they saw their proportion of US-manufactured imports rise almost 30 percent between 2018 and 2020, in comparison with China which saw its share of the market fall by around 15 percent.

Given all these headwinds for globalization, it might be considered that there would also be a very strong trend for nearshoring, benefiting all countries, for instance, in Latin America. Indeed, as Mauricio Claver-Carone, the president of the Inter-American Development Bank, said, this should be the 'golden era for investment'. However, this is not necessarily the case. For example, between 2018 and 2020 imports of man-ufactured goods from Mexico – a market which would have expected to have been a prime beneficiary of the trade war – to the US stagnated (Stott and Murray, 2022).

What this has shown is that the political and economic environment in many emerging markets is not conducive and, indeed, can be openly hostile to foreign investment. This has meant that for many countries the post-pandemic recovery has been slow and this, combined with wage increases (especially those fuelled by inflation) and low public investment in infra-structure, has nullified any competitive advantage which they may have had over Chinese competitors.

DIVERGENT TRADE POLICIES LEAD TO FRAGMENTATION OF THE WEST

Although it is possible to characterize the present geo-political situation as 'the West versus China', that is to ignore the many tensions which exist between Western allies which are, after all, competing economies. As will be discussed in Chapter 6, many of the USA's natural allies in Asia are resentful that the ban on the export of advanced technology to China has prevented them from trading with their biggest market. Meanwhile, many in Europe reject the premise that they must slavishly follow the lead of the United States as regards security policy, despite the fact that they have relied on its military protection since the end of World War II.

Whilst committed in most respects to a similar set of values, members of the 'global West', as it has been termed, seem increasingly divergent in their approach to trade matters. Speaking to press after a European Council meeting in October 2022 at which relations with China were discussed, Olaf Schulz, Germany's chancellor, commented, 'The EU prides itself on being a union interested in global trade and it does not side with those who promote deglobalization' (Brzozowski, 2022). This was taken as a jibe at the US attempts to control trade with China. China is, after all, Germany's largest trading partner with combined imports and exports in excess of €245bn and it is understandable that at a time when another key element of its economic success – cheap energy from Russia – has been disrupted, the government is unwilling to commit to a course of action which would inflict further damage. It is estimated that 1 million jobs depend directly on China–German trade and many more people are employed indirectly (von Hein, 2022).

However, Germany's dependency on China goes even deeper. Whilst markets such as the US also rely on Chinese imports, German companies – not least in the automotive sector – have invested heavily in the Chinese economy itself. Germany's foreign direct investment in China amounts to 14 percent of its total, in contrast to just 2 percent of America's. BMW, Mercedes-Benz, Volkswagen and BASF accounted for a third of all investments in China over the past four years. Revenues generated by the Chinese market also account for a much higher proportion of German multinationals' turnover than equivalent US blue chips. This shows a major difference between offshoring production and sourcing strategies. Given the billions of dollars invested in Chinese manufacturing plants by German companies and their reliance on the domestic market, there is little appetite to criticize Chinese government policy or to heed Western politicians' calls to reduce their exposure on grounds of security. Companies which have engaged with the Chinese market through a contract manufacturer, for instance, or with Chinese manufacturers on looser contractual ties, have the ability to adopt 'China plus' strategies or leave the market completely if other options exist. Many German companies do not have this freedom given their previous 'all in' approach and their wholehearted backing of their government's 'change through trade' policy which failed so spectacularly in the case of Russia.

Germany's commitment to China, and China's version of globalization, is not shared by its other European partners. In fact, growing tensions are threatening to break apart any consensus on trade policy. President Macron has long been an advocate of 'strategic autonomy', a fact emphasized by giving ministers in his government responsibility for areas such as 'industrial sovereignty' and 'food sovereignty'. Addressing French diplomats in October 2022 he commented that, '...the pandemic broke apart production chains. It re-regionalized, and sometimes renationalized certain production chains. And I believe that it deglobalized a significant portion of global production for the long term. That is the first reality that fractures the international economic order, whether we like it or not' (Macron, 2022).

This 'dirigiste' political approach, supporting national heroes and erecting barriers to foreign companies in the national interest, is more akin to the United States' security-driven intervention in global markets than the multilateral 'globalization' seemingly favoured by Germany. There are also fears in some quarters in Europe that France's promotion of strategic autonomy is designed to lessen America's influence in Europe and hence allow France to fill any security or economic void.

Whilst President Trump was regarded as no friend by many European politicians, President Biden's administration has done little to rebuild trans-Atlantic bridges. Although some of Trump's tariffs have been removed, many remain and, in addition to this, Biden's Inflation Reduction Act drew accusations from European politicians that the subsequent 'green' subsidies for goods made in the USA would result in unfair competition. Inevitably this also resulted in calls for more subvention for European manufacturers to allow them to compete on equal terms.

CONCLUSION

The fragmentation of supply chains seems inevitable in the current political climate. Neo-liberal dreams of a 'flat world' in which trade fosters growth and promotes democracy have been rejected for a 'Balkanised' structure based instead on domestic political priorities and geo-political ambitions. The US, EU, China and India, four of the world's most powerful trading entities, are, to a lesser or greater degree, turning their back on the WTO, which is regarded by many leaders – both in the West and in the emerging world – as weak, ineffectual and increasingly irrelevant. China has been largely responsible for this, with many in the West resentful over the way in which China has hijacked the global trading regime for its own political and economic ends. 'Wandel durch Handel' was the phrase commonly used in German foreign policy ('change through trade') to justify closer commercial ties with authoritarian regimes such as China and Russia. Unfortunately, the 'change' which has occurred has been the decline of free trade as a result of increasing protectionism, tariffs and subsidies.

REFERENCES

Alkousaa, R (2022) EU in talks with US over new IRA law trade issues, Reuters. Available from https://www.reuters.com/business/eu-talks-with-us-over-new-ira-law-trade- issues-2022-11-03/

Aulakh, G (2017) Government's approval to PMP in assembling mobile parts will boost investment, Economic Times. Available from https://economictimes.indiatimes.com/tech/hardware/governments-approval-to-pmp-in-assembling-mobile-parts-will-boost- investment/

Bacchus, J (2022) Biden and trade at year one: the reign of polite protectionism, Cato Institute. Available from www.cato.org/policy-analysis/biden-trade-year-one

Brzozowski, A (2022) EU leaders wary of dependencies created with China, but far from united, Euractiv. Available from https://www.euractiv.com/section/eu-china/news/eu- leaders-wary-of-dependencies-created-with-china-but-far-from-united/

Cebeci, D (2020) What changes to expect from a Biden presidency on trade and China? Ti Insight. Available from www.ti-insight.com/briefs/what-changes-to-expect-from-a- biden-presidency-on-trade-and-china/

Christensen, R and Hearson, M (2022) The rise of China and contestation in global tax governance, Asia Pacific Business Review, 28:2, 165-186, DOI: 10.1080/13602381.2022.2012992

EPRS (2022) EU strategic autonomy 2013-2023: from concept to capacity, European Parliamentary Research Service. Available from www.europarl.europa.eu/RegData/etudes/BRIE/2022/733589/EPRS_BRI(2022)733589_EN.pdf

EUCCC (2017) China Manufacturing 2025, European Union Chamber of Commerce in China. Available from http://docs.dpaq.de/12007-european_chamber_cm2025-en.pdf

Financial Times (2022) European industry pivots to US as Biden subsidy sends 'dangerous signal', Financial Times, London, 21 November 2022.

Horton, B and Hopewell, K (2021) Lessons from Trump's assault on the World Trade Organization, Chatham House. Available from www.chathamhouse.org/2021/08/lessons-trumps-assault-world-trade-organization

Lobosco, K (2020) Breaking down the costs of Trump's trade war with China, CNN. Available at https://edition.cnn.com/2020/01/14/politics/cost-of-china-tariff-trade-war/ index.html

Macron, E (2022) Speech by the President of the French Republic at the conference of ambassadors, Elysée Palace. Available from www.elysee.fr/en/emmanuel-macron/ 2022/09/01/speech-by-the-president-of-the-french-republic-at-the-conference-of-ambassadors-1

Singh, M (2021) Forget winning, can Amazon survive in India? TechCrunch. Available from https://techcrunch.com/2021/01/25/india-plays-hardball-with-amazon/

Stott, M and Murray, C (2022) Why Mexico is missing its chance to profit from US-China decoupling, Financial Times. Available from www.ft.com/content/7fc2adf0-0577- 4e13-b9a3-218dda2ddd5b

Swaminathan S. Anklesaria Aiyar (2018) India's new protectionism threatens gains from economic reform, Cato Institute. Available from www.cato.org/policy-analysis/indias- new-protectionism-threatens-gains-economic-reform

Swaminathan S. Anklesaria Aiyar (2018a) Davos Forgotten, Modi Is Turning 'Make in India' into 'Protect in India', Times of India, 4 February 2018.

Von Hein, M (2022) Is Germany too dependent on China? Deutsche Welle. Available from www.dw.com/en/is-germanys-economy-too-dependent-on-china

White House (2021) Building resilient supply chains, revitalizing American manufacturing, and fostering broad-based growth, The White House. Available from www.whitehouse. gov/wp-content/uploads/2021/06/100-day-supply-chain-review-report.pdf

3

Subsidies and Their Role in Supply Chain Distortion

INTRODUCTION

Analyses of supply chain management strategies more often than not concentrate on the economic factors involved in geo-spatial distribution decisions. The role of state subsidy in this process is often overlooked, despite billions of dollars of tax-payers' money being spent on incentivizing manufacturers, retailers or logistics companies to base their production facilities, headquarters or distribution centres in a certain region. Warehousing, in particular, often involves highly labour-intensive processes and is regarded as a relatively quick and easy way of stimulating local economies and employment markets. However, the issue of subsidy is not without controversy, as has been highlighted by President Biden's Inflation Reduction Act (IRA). The huge support package contains protectionist measures which have outraged the EU and other countries.

INCENTIVIZING INVESTMENT

The use of subsidies to attract economic investment is a ubiquitous practice undertaken by local, regional and national governments, regardless of political persuasion or whether based in a developed or emerging market. Despite its seeming universality, the practice runs counter to the ethos of open markets and can, in some cases, breach competition legislation such as that applied in the EU or arbitrated by the WTO.

In fact, subsidy is at the heart of the latest disagreement between the EU and the USA. EU administrators believe that the Biden administration's Inflation Reduction Act presents a significant risk in that many European manufacturers will be forced to relocate production to the USA in order to qualify for subsidies. Reported in the *Financial Times*, Germany's Economy Minister, Robert Habeck commented that in effect the subsidies would 'hoover up investments from Europe' (*Financial Times*, 2022), although it is evident that it will have a similar impact on businesses located in Asia. In response, however, the US has doubled down on its proposals, telling the EU that it should increase its own subsidies. If a subsidy war escalates, combined with the protectionist sentiment already seen over the last decade, global trade would be significantly affected. Supply chains will become 'Balkanized' – with the trend towards national and regional, rather than intercontinental, flows of goods.

Even within a country, supply chains can be skewed by subsidies and tax policies. Nowhere has this been more evident than in the US where states have competed against each other to attract the country's biggest online retail platform, Amazon. One lobby organization, Good Jobs First, estimates that states and municipalities have provided Amazon with over $5.1 billion in direct and indirect subsidies and tax breaks. For example:

- Amazon received $124m to locate a warehouse in Niagara County, New York.
- Blount County in Tennessee invested $12m in improving roads to an Amazon warehouse accounted for by a payment 'in lieu of taxes' over 20 years.
- Amazon has also benefited from a so-called 'back door' tax break technique, tax increment financing (TIF). This results in lower costs for developers which are then passed on to occupiers (such as Amazon) through lower rents.

This is not just a feature of the US market. In Europe, Amazon has received local government subsidy packages including in:

- Asturias, Spain ($5.1m)
- Lyon, France ($1.3m)
- Leipzig, Germany ($15.6m)
- Fife, Scotland ($10.44m)

It is believed that Amazon has received subsidies from local or national governments in 13 countries for up to 407 facilities. According to the report by Good Jobs First, '...many of the developing countries where Amazon has large networks of facilities are places widely known for aggressive subsidy use by subnational (i.e., state, provincial, or local) governments' (Thomas et al, 2022).

In Europe, also, the EC's regulatory regime encourages development in poorer regions by allowing local governments to offer state aid. This has helped Amazon reportedly secure subsidy in Poland for the development of facilities although in this case Amazon's distribution strategy has also been influenced by the desire to avoid Germany's more expensive, highly regulated and strike-prone labour market.

It goes without saying that national and local administrators believe that subsidies play an important role in the location of production and distribution facilities. After all, if a country or a region was overwhelmingly attractive for a range of economic, geographic and risk-based reasons, it would not need to offer financial incentives to the company which it wanted to attract. This was, in substance, the point made by the German Finance Minister, Christian Lindmer, in an article for the *FT* (2022) talking about the impact of IRA subsidies, 'We won't prevent European companies disinvesting and moving to the US by entering into a competition for subsidies, but by creating really excellent conditions for investment in Europe'.

It is logical, therefore, that the location of a subsidized facility may be sub-optimal in terms of supply chain as financial

Table 3.1 Factors involved in the location of distribution centres

Logistics attributes	Economic factors	Risk
Proximity to end user	Cost of rental, land and development	Risk of natural disaster
Geographic centrality	Labour availability	Geo-political
Proximity to transport hubs	Labour costs	Industrial disputes
Customer service level required	Skill set	
Transport links	Taxation policy	
Transport frequency	Financial incentives	
Efficiency of customs	ICT infrastructure	
Transport costs		

incentives necessarily demote or at least balance other factors in the decision-making process. These other factors will include *inter alia* land costs, regulations, labour costs, skilled workforce, information and communications technology infrastructure, energy supply and environmental risks in addition to logistics factors, such as road, rail, sea and air links (see Figure 3.1).

Whilst government investment is expected to create the business conditions in which industry can prosper, supporting individual companies is much more controversial due to the way in which it can distort markets. However, politicians find it difficult to resist the temptation of awarding subsidies or tax-breaks to big new employers if they think it will bring positive public relations. A less cynical view perhaps is that governments – national and local – have a responsibility to promote growth at the same time as ensuring economic resilience. The latter factor has resulted in the eye-watering amounts of money being promised to semiconductor companies to establish wafer fabrication plants in Western markets to counter the perceived Chinese threat to Taiwan (see Chapter 6).

TAX POLICY AND THE IMPACT OF THE MINIMUM TAX TREATY

As well as financial incentives, an advantageous taxation policy is also an important lever used by governments to attract
production and distribution operations, again with the hope of
stimulating economic activity and job growth. Recent moves
at an intergovernmental level have sought to address what
has been seen by many as a 'race to the bottom' as countries
compete to attract investment from multinationals. However,
as we will see, this initiative may well be counter-productive
for emerging markets forced to compete for investment on a
non-fiscal basis. Also, popular, and unaffected by this recent
change in taxation policy, is the development of free/foreign
trade zones which offer advantageous terms to the companies
which base their production or warehousing facilities within
them. For many countries, such as the UAE, these have proved
the cornerstone of a supply chain vision which has transformed
a relative backwater into a global logistics hub. But tariffs and
taxes can also be used as a stick rather than as a carrot. This
is the thinking behind the EU's Carbon Border Adjustment
Mechanism (CBAM) which seeks to influence the behaviour
of global manufacturers by penalizing them for using heavily
polluting suppliers in less carbon-efficient parts of the world
(see Chapter 11).

The minimum tax treaty

In 2022, 139 countries signed up to a 'minimum tax treaty'
with the express aim of making multinational companies pay
higher levels of tax based on a new, 'more equitable' calcula-
tion. Politicians and tax authorities have become concerned
that legacy tax regulations have not been able to keep pace
with the digital economy which has allowed global platforms,
such as Amazon, to pay little or no tax in some of their largest
markets. However, it would be wrong to think that the treaty

only affects companies working in what might be termed the 'metaverse'. It has been designed to impact all sectors of the economy and therefore may have consequences for supply chain structuring.

There are two 'pillars' to the minimum tax treaty (Gaspar, 2022).

- Pillar 1: A proportion of the profits of multinational companies will now be taxed on the basis of the location of their customers, rather than on where the business is registered for tax purposes.
- Pillar 2: A minimum corporate tax rate of 15 percent will be introduced, putting what the International Monetary Fund (IMF) calls a 'floor' on competition between tax authorities.

Whilst much attention has been paid to the tax-raising effects of the treaty and the reduction of wasteful tax incentives, less attention has been paid to the impact which it will have on supply chain organization.

Many emerging markets offer multinational manufacturers tax-break incentives (such as tax holidays, preferential tax rates, tax credits, investment allowances or income exemptions) to locate their production in their country, even though the official rate of corporation tax may be much higher than the proposed minimum of 15 percent (Readhead et al, 2021). Under Pillar 2, these countries would have to 'top up' the tax with a surcharge, reducing or eliminating one of the key reasons for a multinational's presence in the market.

It has been argued that the tax treaty will result in developing countries increasing their tax take as the 'floor' will be raised in all markets. However, if the tax rate is no longer a country's competitive advantage, manufacturers will base their location decisions on factors such as speed to market, labour costs, infrastructure etc. This is undoubtedly a positive development but one which in the short term will have ramifications for developing countries which need to invest time and money on developing these other attributes.

Some economists believe that the inevitable consequence of the tax treaty will be to reduce investment in low-tax countries (Vaitilingam, 2021). In Europe, those with seemingly most to lose, if this is indeed the case, include Ireland, Hungary and Bulgaria; in the Middle East, Qatar and the UAE; in Latin America, Chile and Paraguay; and in Asia, Macao (Bray, 2021). The Irish government, which originally opposed the deal, estimated that it would lose out by between €800m and €2bn a year in corporate tax revenue. Although much of this relates to the profits of digital giants such as Facebook, Google and Yahoo, Ireland also acts as a major manufacturing location for the pharma sector (e.g., Pfizer) and high tech (e.g., Intel). It is too early to be seen whether the increased tax rate will lead to an exodus from the market but, if it does, it will have significant implications for the associated supply chains.

Free trade zones

According to think tank the Royal United Service Institute (RUSI), free or foreign trade zones (FTZs) 'form the backbone of global supply chains and are the lubricant to the cogwheels of globalisation' (Fuller, 2019). It goes on to define them as:

- geographically delineated areas considered to be outside of the normal customs area
- having a management authority that can be public, private or mixed
- offering special benefits in exchange for locating within the zone.

As merchandise is not being formally imported into a country, no duties are payable until and unless the goods are transferred out of the FTZ and into free circulation. As well as savings on duty, this also means that various value adding processes can be performed on an intermediate good without customs processes slowing each stage of the supply chain. This results in shorter cycle times, increased inventory turn and better traceability of stock.

FTZs allow manufacturers to gain relief from inverted tariffs, that is, in certain cases, intermediate goods are taxed at a higher rate than finished products. This can mean that manufacturers producing goods in a certain jurisdiction end up paying higher levels of tax than competitors importing goods. For example, tyres can attract tariffs of 4 percent on import into the US. When fitted to a car and transferred to US commerce, the duty becomes 2.5 percent as they are part of a finished product (Thomson Reuters, 2019).

FTZs also exempt importers from duty on:

- re-exports to a foreign country
- waste or scrap loss
- zone-to-zone transfers.

Other benefits include:

- 'single window' services (obviating the regulatory need for importers to deal with multiple government agencies)
- tax holidays
- free movement of people.

Most developed and emerging countries have established FTZs, amongst them the USA and China, as a way of encouraging foreign direct investment (FDI) and stimulating knowledge exchange.

China provides the most compelling evidence of the success which a country can have in attracting investment from global manufacturers through taxation policies, and FTZs have been an important element in its aggressive economic development policy. Since the 1980s China has used various types of FTZs to integrate its economy into global value chains (GVCs) firstly by encouraging the growth of labour-intensive industries within special economic zones and then subsequently directing incentives towards higher value, more capital and technology-intensive sectors. In terms of supply chain geography, the FTZs were initially based in coastal areas especially in ports. However, they were then established in regional centres and extended inland to Western regions as part of government economic expansion policy. Over the years these areas have evolved from providing simple bonded warehousing services to those which today provide comprehensive logistics, after-sale services and research and development – 'diversified economic centres for finance, shipping, trading, professional services, cultural and social services' (CAREC, 2022).

Obviously, FTZs are just one incentive available to governments to attract investment to specific areas. However, they were important in China's successful efforts to gain business from Japan and the 'Asian tigers' in the 1980s and 1990s: stimulating growth in the Pearl and Yangtze River Deltas in the 2000s and subsequently western parts of the country.

Now that sourcing goods from China has become more expensive due to rising labour costs, tariffs and, most recently, the government's zero-Covid policy, manufacturers have sought suppliers in alternative markets. Consequently, in order to attract the investment which has become 'disengaged' from China, Southeast Asian governments have established development policies, including the expansion of FTZs. Vietnam, for instance, has 18 coastal economic zones and 325 state-supported industrial parks across the country (Tetra, 2022). Its largest, Dinh Vu - Cat Hai Economic Zone, offers an income-tax holiday for the first four years and a reduced tax rate for an additional nine years.

Likewise, FTZs are being used as a way of encouraging reshoring in the West. They have been especially effective in the US where, first established in the Great Depression of

1934, 197 FTZs employ over 480,000 people. In 2021, the value of merchandise imported into FTZs leapt by a third to $836 billion. Production operations received $466 billion of this total with the remainder going into warehousing or distribution. Domestic inputs into FTZs increased at a higher rate and the total proportion of US components used overall in assembled products rose to 77 percent from 74 percent (FTZB, 2022). FTZs have become tax-efficient manufacturing hubs, allowing imported intermediates to be combined with domestically produced components to take advantage of lower duty rates. This became particularly important during the West Coast port congestion when importers were forced to increase inventory levels to ensure a consistent supply of product to US consumers. This would mean significant cash-flow issues, especially in light of the Trump/Biden 'trade remedy' tariffs, if these duties have to be paid up-front before the goods were sold.

The UK has become the latest country to establish FTZs (Freeports as they have been dubbed due to their coastal location). Proponents believe that they will pull in badly needed investment, using spare capacity at many of the UK's ports, especially those located in close proximity to manufacturing hubs such as Nissan in Sunderland. Critics believe that they won't be as effective as those in the US due to the lower levels of tariffs which the UK levies. Others believe that they will result in purely re-distributing existing UK production capacity rather than stimulating growth. If this is the case (and one of the government's aims is to help more deprived areas of the country where many of the Freeports are based), this will have the effect of shifting supply chains from a focus on the Southeast to other parts of the country. This will have implications for logistics requirements.

Perhaps the most egregious example of how a country can use FTZs to transform its economy is the United Arab Emirates (UAE). In conjunction with investment in transport, ICT, financial and energy infrastructure, the creation of 45 FTZs has helped the country to diversify away from a reliance on hydrocarbons to become a broad-based global trade hub. In 2021, 60,600 companies were operating in UAE's FTZs. As well as the preferential tariff regime, another advantage for international investors has been that companies could retain 100 percent foreign ownership whilst based in an FTZ as opposed to requiring a joint venture with an Emirati business if operating 'on-shore'. The best-known FTZ is the Jebel Ali Free Zone (Jafza) which accounts for almost a quarter of all foreign investment in the country. The UAE now serves the whole of the Middle East region as well as India, Africa and parts of Central Asia. Through investment and policy, it has created a new market, serving a region which would otherwise have been less accessible to global value chains, thereby stimulating economic growth.

Environmental taxes on supply chains

Whilst FTZs may be one of the 'carrots' used to attract invest-ment through such measures as the deferment of the pay-ment of duties, taxation policy can also be used as a 'stick' to achieve governmental aims. With the environment now regarded as a priority, administrators have been keen to levy taxes on highly polluting supply chains as a lever to change corporate behaviour. 'As more environmental externalities, whether carbon related or not, are identified and written into the green legislation, supply chains will be subject to taxes and pricing measures at multiple places in the supply chains', com-mented Alenka Turnsek, EMEIA Sustainability Tax Leader at accountant Ernst & Young. 'The environmental tax and regu-lation legislation landscape is increasingly complex and frag-mented' (Turnsek, 2021).

In summary, government levies will make highly polluting supply chains less competitive, 'levelling the playing field' for manufacturers which source goods from less carbon-emitting suppliers or those using cleaner forms of transport. As well as embodied carbon within the supply chain, policies are also being brought forward to address issues such as:

- shipping emissions
- packaging reduction
- water preservation
- biodiversity.

The full range and extent of so-called 'green' legislation is discussed in Chapter 11 including the EU's forthcoming Carbon Border Adjustment Mechanism (CBAM). However, in summary, green legislation as it affects the supply chain will lead to a search for 'value' in terms of economic, environmental and societal impact. This will have implications in terms of where the value-adding process will take place. New processes will develop and others will be migrated to regions or countries which have a lower carbon footprint or better environmental and ethical practices.

There is little doubt that taxation policy will play a much bigger role in company strategy in the future. This will involve identifying these new costs and changing supply chain strategy accordingly. For this to be possible, companies will need much greater visibility of the origin of the intermediate goods sourced from their suppliers, and indeed, their suppliers' suppliers. At the other end of the supply chain, they will also need to have in place a strategy to deal with circularity and end of life for their products.

As Ernst & Young comments, 'The tax function has a significant role to play in supply chain change. If a company doesn't know its environmental tax footprint, or how it's set to change, it may be exposed to unnecessary costs or it could under-utilize tax incentives on its transformation journey' (Turnsek, 2021).

CONCLUSION

Subsidy, tax policy and free trade zones are significant factors in the location of logistics facilities, key nodes in supply chains. The use of incentives and tax breaks has created another layer of complexity in the development of distribution networks which can lead to economic inefficiencies. The 'minimum tax treaty' may also have unintended consequences which will disadvantage developing countries, at least until they are able to improve market environment and infrastructure. Environmental taxes will also have cost implications for manufacturers and retailers, but administrators believe that this will lead to the development of optimized supply chains from the perspective of carbon emissions.

REFERENCES

Bray, S (2021) Corporate tax rates around the world, 2021, Tax Foundation. Available from https://taxfoundation.org/publications /corporate-tax-rates-around-the-world/

CAREC (2022) The development experience of China's special economic zones, and practice of free zones, Central Asia Regional Economic Cooperation Program. Available from www .carecprogram.org/uploads/Developing-Sustainable-Economic-Zones_Session-3-Group-2_PRC-Pan-Li_Eng.pdf

Financial Times (2022) European industry pivots to US as Biden subsidy sends 'dangerous signal', Financial Times, London 21 November 2022.

FTZB (2022) 83rd Annual report of the Foreign-trade Zones Board, Foreign-trade Zones Board. Available from https://www.trade .gov/sites/default/files/2022-08/AR-2021_0.pdf

Fuller, C (2019) Transparency in the backbone of global supply chains: foreign trade zones, RUSI. Available from https://rusi .org/explore-our-research/publications/commentary/transparency -backbone-global-supply-chains-foreign-trade-zones

Gaspar, V et al (2022) Tax coordination can lead to a fairer, greener global economy, International Monetary Fund. Available from www.imf.org/en/Blogs/Articles/2022/04/ 12/blog041222-sm2022 -fm-ch2

Readhead, A et al (2021) The end of tax incentives: how will a global minimum tax affect tax incentives regimes in developing countries? International Institute for Sustainable Development. Available from www.iisd.org/itn/en/2021/10/07/the-end- of-tax-incentives -how-will-a-global-minimum-tax-affect-tax-incentives-regimes -in- developing-countries-alexandra-readhead-thomas-lassourd -howard-mann/

Tetra (2022) Vietnam free trade zones, Tetra Consultants. Available from www. tetraconsultants.com/jurisdictions/register-company -in-vietnam/vietnam-free-trade- zones/

Thomas, K et al (2022) Amazon.com's Hidden Worldwide Subsidies, Good Jobs First and UNI Global Union. Available from https:// goodjobsfirst.org/wp-content/uploads/2022/   07/Amazon.coms -Hidden-Worldwide-Subsidies.pdf

Thomson Reuters (2019) Building the business case for foreign-trade zones, Thomson Reuters. Available from https://tax

.thomsonreuters.com/content/dam/ewp-m/docu ments/tax/en/pdf /ebooks/building-the-business-case-for-ftz-ebook.pdf

Turnsek, A (2021) Statutory tax penalties and incentives around sustainability and the environment are forcing a radical rethink of global supply chains, Ernst & Young. Available from www .ey.com/en_gl/tax/how-tax-is-influencing-the-design-of-sust ainable-supply-chains

Vaitilingam, R (2021) Would a global minimum corporate tax rate end the 'race to the bottom'? Chicago Booth Review. Available from https://www.chicagobooth.edu/review/would-global-minimum -corporate-tax-rate-end-race-bottom

4

Friends and Enemies

The Rise of Ally Sourcing

INTRODUCTION

Heightening tensions between the US, its Western allies and China are shaping the development of supply chains based on geo-political allegiances rather than economic logic, a trend known as 'ally' or 'friend' sourcing. Whilst such a development may seem necessary from a security perspective, it will mean that supply chains become more inefficient and expensive, with implications for Western businesses and consumers.

The geo-political landscape has become even more complicated by Russia's invasion of Ukraine. Sanctions have pushed Russia into what could be termed as the 'Sino-sphere': supplying oil and natural resources to China in return for a range of high-tech and consumer goods. This is a major shift from before the war, when Russia was integrated into European, rather than Chinese, supply chains.

Globalization could be said to be playing a role in its own downfall. The re-distribution of wealth and trade from the West to emerging markets has empowered ambitious countries such as China and Russia, destabilizing engrained economic structures and disrupting political stasis. However, it has also altered the balance of power on a regional basis. Turkey has been one such beneficiary of offshoring (near-sourcing in its case). However, instead of embracing Western values and free-market doctrine, it has adopted increasingly autocratic and dirigiste policies.

A NEW VISION FOR GLOBALIZATION?

The war in Ukraine has increased pressure on a global trading regime already creaking under the stress of a sidelined World Trade Organization; increased protectionism; deteriorating US–China relations and, of course, Covid-19. Whilst there are still many who promote the economic benefits of 'free trade', this argument is becoming more difficult to make due to a fracturing of any consensus which may have previously existed.

The pursuit of 'open and unfettered' access to international markets has naively allowed countries such as China to promote their soft power and influence through trade and investment. China's Belt and Road Initiative (BRI) is a case in point. Its investment in transport infrastructure in emerging markets has given it huge influence in countries throughout Asia, Africa and Latin America. European and US governments over the past 20 years, beguiled by the riches of China's domestic market, have, until recently, been blind to the Chinese government's barely concealed ambition to use globalization as a means to a political end. Some may say that globalization has been hijacked to create a Sino-centric trading network, acting as a conduit for political leverage. The West has only itself to blame. After the Great Recession of 2008/9, many institutions and banks withdrew from emerging markets leaving a vacuum of finance. This allowed China to step into the void and resulted in a pivot eastwards by many countries desperate for the investment to continue their development plans and bitter towards the West.

Only recently have the EU and the US attempted to address the growing influence of China. At the 2021 G7 meeting, the Build Back Better World (B3W) Initiative was launched, aimed at 'narrowing the $40 trillion developing country infrastructure gap' by 2035 and providing an alternative to China's 'problematic lending practices' (CNBC, 2021). Unlike China's financing deals, there would be fewer political strings attached.

The US has also sought to exploit political tensions between the two giants of the developing world, India and China. India, unlike neighbours Pakistan, Nepal and Sri Lanka, refused to join the BRI due to worries over its territorial integrity. The US and, more widely, the G7 hope that an alliance of democratic countries can be created to counter the expansion of China and in return facilitate the transfer of technology, skill development and finance. However, India's stance on Russia's invasion of Ukraine will provide little encouragement that this 'democratic alliance' is more than an aspiration.

POLITICIZED SUPPLY CHAINS MAKE
LATIN AMERICA A KEY BATTLEGROUND

The heightening tensions between the US and China have raised the prospect of the development of two distinct supply chain hegemonies, in which competing suppliers, strategic technologies and critical components are kept discrete for reasons of national security. However, given the complexity of international relationships, especially between the West and the developing world, it is inevitable that many emerging countries will not want to be coerced into a paradigm where they have to embrace one side or the other.

Latin America is a case in point and the region represents a major headache for the Biden administration. Many local politicians, even some closely aligned with the US, feel that they have been ignored by their neighbour for too long and consequently have been open to China's offer of funds and access to its market, regardless of the political provisos. In fact, over the past decade China has replaced the US as the major trade partner for the majority of countries in the region, with the exception of Mexico.

China's Belt and Road Initiative has provided a huge source of investment and 19 out of 24 Latin American countries have signed up in one form or another. This has meant that many supply chains have become controlled by Chinese companies and businesses from countries which have resisted the temptation of Chinese money often find themselves being 'locked out' of lucrative contracts.

The massive sums invested do not mean that the US has lost all its political and military influence in the region. However, many of its neighbours are unwilling to make economic sacrifices for the US when they have little idea of what they can expect in return. What's more, China doesn't just offer commercial opportunities. As part of a 'hearts and minds' campaign it donated millions of vaccines to Latin America throughout the Covid-19 crisis as well as personal protective equipment (PPE), winning significant political goodwill (De Avila et al, 2022).

Despite this, China's economic sway is still largely limited to infrastructure building and the sourcing of raw materials, whilst the US has much more influence in the high-tech and communications technology sectors. This is where key supply chain battles of the future are likely to be fought. For example, former president Trump agreed a deal with Ecuador that would enable the country to pay down its debt to China, as well as allowing investment in its oil and infrastructure sectors, so long as it did not allow Chinese tech company, Huawei, to participate in the development of its 5G network. However, given Huawei's strong presence in many other parts of the region, this particular supply chain battle may already have been lost.

It is not just China which the US has to worry about. Russia and Iran are also making overtures to governments in the region. Russia, for instance, has threatened to deploy military forces in Cuba, Venezuela and Nicaragua partly in response to the international community's condemnation of the invasion of Ukraine and partly due to a longer-standing strategy of projecting its power into 'America's backyard'. India and Turkey are also pursuing their own agendas and, along with the other emerging international powers, are promoting a 'multipolar' rather than 'unipolar' world as being in their best interests. As Spanish foreign affairs think tank, Real Instituto Elcano, put it, these countries are, '...challenging US hegemony and trying to displace it economically, technologically, militarily and commercially [from the region]'.

The Biden administration is aware of these risks and has attempted to re-boot its relationship with its southern neighbours through the 'Americas Partnership for Economic Prosperity' initiative. However, this got off to a rocky start when it launched at a conference in Los Angeles in June 2022 when several heads of state were either excluded or stayed away. Biden's plans include increased roles for the Inter-American Development Bank and the creation of new jobs through clean energy technology. However, this raises the question, will the US be happy to share technologies with Latin American businesses which may also work with the Chinese?

The issues which the US faces in Latin America will inevitably be replicated in Africa and Asia where China's influence is already endemic. The US has considerable economic, political and military power, of course, but it, and the West as a whole, has already ceded much ground to its geo-political rivals. Investment by Western banks in emerging markets shrank during the Covid-19 crisis at rates not seen since records began in 2005 and this vacuum is likely to be filled by Chinese money, only increasing its political influence (Wheatley, 2022). With this as the background, the development of ally-sourcing strategies – the creation of secure supply chains involving known and validated suppliers located in friendly countries – may only act to exclude and alienate emerging markets further, increasing the gap between the technology haves and have nots.

RUSSIA JOINS THE 'SINO-SPHERE'

The trade and finance sanctions imposed by much of the international community on Russia following its invasion of Ukraine in February 2022 have resulted in its exclusion from the majority of Western supply chains. This has necessarily forced Russia to a pivot towards countries which remain supportive of the Putin government or at least seek to retain neutrality.

Of these countries, China is by far the most important and the increasingly close relationship between the two partners resulted in a surge in trade immediately after the invasion. China customs data for 2022 indicated that bilateral trade increased by 30 percent to $190 billion. (He, 2023)

Whilst Russian exports are predominantly commodities such as oil, gas, soybean, timber and vegetable oils, imports from China are higher value add including mechanical products, mobile phones, transport equipment and consumer products.

Russia's need for high-tech products has become critical given US-led export controls put in place in February 2022, which prevented the sale of semiconductors, information and telecoms equipment, electronics and computers to Russia. Korea and Japan signed up to the embargo, and Taiwan is effectively bound by its constraints due to the application of the US 'foreign direct product' rule. This means that the export of any chips (and many other products) made using US equipment or software is banned to proscribed countries, now including Russia.

It is reported that these controls have already had a far-reaching impact on the Russian economy, especially in its more advanced manufacturing sectors. For example, its aerospace industry has been hard hit with the delay of the flagship airline project, the MC-21. Car manufacturers, already facing chip supply chain shortages, are now in crisis, including national vehicle maker AvtoVAZ. After a complete cessation, it was able to start production of one model in June 2022 but only after it adapted the vehicle to include, as it commented, '…as much localization as possible, excluding the effect of imported components' shortage' (Russiart, 2022). In effect, this means stripping out latest technologies and regressing to those employed in previous generations of cars.

The recent invasion of Ukraine may have led to a sweeping trade embargo by the West, but some sanctions had already been in place following Russia's 2014 incursion into the Crimea. This had resulted in an earlier pivot to China, Taiwan and Malaysia from German, Italian and French electronics suppliers, although Russia's ambitious plans for developing its own high-tech sector have been almost entirely unsuccessful (Gross, 2022).

China is likely to play an important role in the future supply of semiconductor chips to Russia, but the US has already warned the country against any breach of agreed export controls. Experts believe that regulations have been adhered to so far but worry that this may not continue much longer given Russia's desperation (Chorzempa, 2022). Publicly, the Chinese government is unhappy about the pressure being exerted by the US, and its Ministry of Commerce has warned that if companies comply with the sanctions, they would risk being placed on its 'Unreliable Entity List'. Despite this, China itself relies heavily on US technology and so will be reticent about blatantly ignoring controls. This seems to be evident in the much lower levels of export growth from China to Russia seen in the first half of 2022 – there was no stampede from Chinese companies to 'backfill' the vacuum created by the lack of Western exports, especially if this means running foul of Western sanctions.

Russia's relationship with India

China is not the only country to provide support to Russia in the face of Western opposition. India too has rejected calls from the US and Europe to back sanctions and, as a result, has become an important market for Russian oil. Before the invasion, only a small volume was exported to India due to the cost of transportation. However, this has rapidly changed due to India's reliance on oil imports and the increase in the global price of energy which is already having an impact on the economy in terms of inflation.

Therefore, the prospect of a cheap source of oil from Russia has been too tempting to turn down, despite Western pressure. Figures in January 2023 show that India is importing over a million barrels of oil a day from Russia, making up more than a quarter of its energy imports (LiveMint, 2023). India's relationship with Russia is long-standing, which makes it unlikely that this energy policy will change anytime soon. In any case, if India looked to source its oil from global markets this would only increase pressure on the oil price – some analysts think by as much as $10 a barrel (Mody, 2022). However, there are concerns that Russian oil, refined in India, may well make its way back into Europe. Oil from various sources can be blended, hiding its origins.

The import of oil is not the only way in which the two countries are collaborating. An agreement between Russia, India and Iran as well as a regional alliance of countries, including Central Asian republics, has facilitated the development of a transport corridor allowing containers to be shipped by rail from Russia through Iran and on to India by sea. India has significantly backed the scheme investing over $2 billion, a proportion of which has involved the construction of infrastructure in Iran (Wani, 2023).

New finance mechanisms

It is not only the physical element of supply chains which is being re-structured. Russia is also looking to China for help in developing alternatives to SWIFT, the system which underpins much of global finance. Since the invasion of Ukraine, Russian banks have been banned from its use, and although Russia has previously developed its own system (post-Crimean incursion), the SPFS, this has only ever been used domestically.

In future, the SPFS could be linked with China's own yuan-backed financial messaging system allowing for the more efficient transfer of funds between traders based in the two countries. A spokesman for the Russian Foreign Ministry said in April 2022, 'It is clear that we are going through a period of adaptation. We need to find possibilities to build supply chains in the new conditions, financial mechanisms for interaction, to ensure settlements in national currencies. This requires some time and effort. And this is what our countries are now actively engaged in' (Tass, 2022). However, China's system itself is very limited and there would be political pushback from the US and its Western allies if China were seen to be helping Russia flout sanctions. Russia's relatively small volume of transactions on the system may not make the subsequent political fallout worthwhile.

TURKEY: FRIEND OR FOE?

Turkey's increasing economic and political influence provides a powerful example of how the impact of globalization can have unintended consequences for international relations. The Ankara Agreement, signed in 1963, was intended to provide a road map to Turkey's full accession to the then European Economic Community (EEC). Whilst full membership is now a remote possibility, a customs union has existed between the two parties since 1996 which was seen at the time as an interim step towards this goal.

Since Turkey's early integration into wider regional and global supply chains, the economy has grown rapidly. It managed to shrug off the Great Recession of 2008 in contrast to many other emerging markets and even sustained growth throughout much of the Covid-19 crisis. Multiple currency devaluations and rampant inflation have done little to take the gloss off its success story, confounding many Western observers.

One of President Erdogan's key fiscal policies is to retain very low interest rates even though inflation in 2022 reached an eye-watering 83 percent, a 24-year high, and the currency exchange rate against the US dollar reached an all-time low (Pitel, 2022). One of the reasons behind this ongoing policy is to increase the attractiveness of the country's exports and this seems to be having an effect. Exports grew by 12 percent in dollar terms to reach a record high in 2022 (Butler and Tuncay, 2023).

In April 2022, the Turkish government published its 30-year 'Transport and Logistics Master Plan 2053' which committed to an investment of $197.9 billion in the rail, road, maritime and air transport and communications sectors. The government believes that the investments will contribute more than $1 trillion to GDP, $1.36 trillion to production and create employment for 27.7 million people (MTI, 2022).

Turkey has become one of Europe's most important centres for automotive production, deeply integrated within the region's parts and finished vehicle supply chains. Since the beginning of the global pandemic in 2020, the sector has benefited from China's zero-Covid policy which has resulted in many vehicle and parts manufacturers switching to Turkish suppliers during periods of lockdown.

However, whilst many believed that increased economic development would naturally result in a more Westernized society, embracing democracy and liberal values, this has been far from the case. The rise of an authoritarian government led by President Erdogan has eliminated any hope of further integration with the EU. In effect, the fruits of globalization have enabled Turkey to pursue a foreign policy uninfluenced by policy overtures from Brussels or Washington. This has led to the development of friendly, albeit capricious, relationships with countries such as Russia and Iran, much to the angst of the Western powers. This despite Turkey remaining a long-standing NATO ally and still, in name at least, an EU accession candidate country. Turkey, for instance, led the buying of Russian crude oil ahead of EU sanctions which came into place in December 2022 and at the same time agreed a deal with Iran for gas exports.

Turkey's non-alignment stance on Russia is being regarded with increasing concern by the EU. According to Nacho Sanchez Amor, a Spanish Social Democrat who is the European Parliament's rapporteur on Turkey, 'It is one thing not to join the sanctions against Russia and quite another to help Russia evade them' (Ertan, 2022). Exports from Turkey to Russia have grown significantly since the invasion as have exports from the EU to Turkey, which the EU believes is a clear sign of circumvention of sanctions. The flow of goods to Turkey is impossible to control as they are officially in free circulation due to the Customs Union treaty. Consequently, Turkey is being seen as Russia's European 'backdoor'.

Turkey's fractious relationship with neighbouring Greece is also of concern and perhaps offers the biggest threat to supply chains. Although tensions go back centuries, relations have worsened in recent years revolving around maritime boundaries, the dispute nature of exclusive economic zones, the future of Cyprus and the discovery of potential gas reserves in the eastern Mediterranean. The deterioration of relations has dragged other countries into the dispute. France, Egypt, Cyprus and the UAE have offered their support to Greece whilst Libya has entered into a strategic alliance with Turkey, providing validation for the latter's maritime claims (Dalay, 2021). Any escalation – including the possibility of incursions by Turkey's armed forces – could result in not only military retaliation by Greece, but in trade sanctions levied by the EU. This would inevitably be counterproductive given the existing high levels of supply chain integration between the trade bloc and Turkey. It might be argued that such interdependence would lessen the possibility of any conflict. However, the case could also be made that President Erdogan will gamble that the EU would not want to take any steps which would result in significant self-harm to key European supply chains such as automotive, fashion and electronics.

Turkey's location as a global, low-cost manufacturing hub on the edge of Europe makes it a hugely valuable resource for the European economy. Turkey will benefit from global manufacturers diversifying their supplier base away from China, especially if government plans to invest in its logistics and transport infrastructure are realized. However, Western manufacturers and retailers must be aware of the exposure of their supply chains to the geo-political risks emanating from President Erdogan's repressive domestic policies and his willingness to engage with the West's adversaries.

CONCLUSION

Globalization has empowered many emerging countries to challenge existing Western hegemonies. China has extended its power and influence globally through its Belt and Road Initiative, funding infrastructure investment in Asia, Latin America and Africa through a series of loans. By doing so it has created a Sino-sphere, posing a clear threat to the USA. In response, the USA has attempted to build a coalition of like-minded allies, a closed community within which technologies can be shared and sourced without risk of sustaining China's military development. However, forcing countries to choose between one camp and the other is unpopular and unlikely to be successful, as is playing out in Latin America.

Russia's invasion of Ukraine and its subsequent exclusion from Western trading networks has resulted in its forced pivot eastwards to China and to a lesser degree India (and other 'non-aligned' economies). This has consolidated the trend towards dual supply chains.

As supply chains become increasingly politicized and 'weaponized', the environment is set to get a lot more compli-cated and expensive for global manufacturers. The next chapter examines in detail how the bifurcation of supply chains is already occurring through a detailed case study of the impact of US legislation on Chinese high-tech manufacturer, Huawei.

REFERENCES

Butler, D and Tuncay, E (2023) Turkey's exports hit record $254 bln in 2022 – Erdogan, Reuters. Available from www.reuters .com/markets/europe/turkeys-exports-hit-record- 254-bln-2022 -erdogan-2023-01-02/

Chorzempa (2022) Export controls against Russia are working—with the help of China, Peterson Institute for International Economics. Available from www.piie.com/blogs/ realtime-economic-issues -watch/export-controls-against-russia-are-working-help- china

CNBC (2021) US plans January rollout of projects to counter China's Belt and Road Initiative, official says, CNBC. Available from www.cnbc.com/2021/11/09/us-project- aims-to-counter-chinas -belt-and-road-initiative-official.html

De Avila, M, Marti, B, Insanally, R and Trevisan, C (2022) US-China vaccine diplomacy: lessons from Latin America and the Caribbean, Atlantic Council. Available from www. atlanticcouncil.org/in -depth-research-reports/report/us-china-vaccine-diplomacy- lessons-from-latin-america-and-the-caribbean/

Dalay, G (2021) Turkey, Europe, and the eastern Mediterranean: charting a way out of the current deadlock, Brookings Institute. Available from www.brookings.edu/research/ turkey-europe-and -the-eastern-mediterranean-charting-a-way-out-of-the-current - deadlock/

Ertan, N (2022) EU warns Turkey on ties with Russia ahead of Erdogan-Putin meeting, Al Monitor. Available from www.al -monitor.com/originals/2022/10/eu-warns-turkey-ties-   russia -ahead-erdogan-putin-meeting

Gross, A (2022) 'Everything is gone': Russian business hit hard by tech sanctions, Financial Times. Available from www.ft.com/ content/caf2cd3c-1f42-4e4a-b24b-c0ed803a6245

He, L (2023) China's exports plunge as global demand weakens, but trade with Russia hits record high, CNN. Available from https:// edition.cnn.com/2023/01/13/economy/china-   exports-struggle -reopening-2022-intl-hnk/index.html

LiveMint (2023) India's Russian oil imports top 1 million barrels a day in December, LiveMint. Available from www.livemint.com/ industry/energy/indias-russian-oil- imports-top-1-million-barrels -a-day-in-december-11673762196458.html

Mody, S (2022) India isn't likely to stop buying Russian oil any time soon. Here's why, CNBC. Available from https://www.cnbc.com

/2022/07/08/india-isnt-likely-to-stop-   buying-russian-oil-any
-time-soon-heres-why.html

MTI (2022) Turkey's Minister of Transport and Infrastructure H.E.
Adil Karaismailoğlu stated that 'Türkiye's 30-year transport plan
is ready', Ministry of Transport and Infrastructure. Available from
https://www.prnewswire.com/news-releases/turkeys- minister-of
-transport-and-infrastructure-he-adil-karaismailolu-stated-that
-turkiyes- 30-year-transport-plan-is-ready-301520939.html

Pitel, L (2022) Turkish inflation tops 83% as Erdoğan promises more
rate cuts, Financial Times. Available from www.ft.com/content/
d6b86397-5b1a-4f54-a21d-786da4b0abc9

Russiart (2022) 'Ensure the maximum possible localization':
AvtoVAZ resumed car assembly in Togliatti, TellerReport.
Available from www.tellerreport.com/news/2022- 06-08-%E2
%80%9Censure-the-maximum-possible-localization%E2%80
%9D-- avtovaz-resumed-car-assembly-in-togliatti.SkzKLdjCO5
.html

Tass (2022) Russia and China are working on supply chains,
settlements in national currencies – MFA, Tass Russian News
Agency. Available from https://tass.com/economy/1440597

Wani, A (2023) Slow, Not Steady: Assessing the Status of India-
Eurasia Connectivity Projects, Observer Research Foundation.
Available from www.orfonline.org/research/assessing-the-status
-of-india-eurasia-connectivity-projects/

Wheatley, J (2022) Emerging markets hit by record streak of
withdrawals by foreign investors, Financial Times. Available from
www.ft.com/content/35969b19-86db-4197- a419-b4a761094e9a

5

Weaponizing High-Tech Supply Chains

Huawei vs The West

INTRODUCTION

The US government's attempts to exclude Huawei from the development of 5G networks, both in the US as well as in many other countries, is creating huge uncertainty over the continued viability of advanced electronics global supply chains. Whilst Huawei is presently at the epicentre of regulators' concerns over potential China-originating security breaches, even rivals such as Nokia and Ericsson are facing scrutiny over the use of China-made components. Some commentators have called these efforts 'weaponizing the supply chain' (Farrell and Newman, 2022) or, in other words, a high-tech supply chain cold war. This in turn is impacting on global supply chain structures and could have a long-lasting impact on economic and technological development.

'A NATIONAL EMERGENCY'

Since 2018, the US government has passed a number of laws aimed at marginalizing Huawei, the world's largest manufacturer of telecoms equipment. Not only has it banned the company's components from US networks and pressured its allies to do the same, but it has also prohibited the use of any US technology in its products. Former president Trump declared the situation a 'National Emergency'.

At the heart of the matter, the US sees Huawei as an extension of the Chinese state's military, providing equipment and parts to 5G networks worldwide whilst at the same time building 'backdoors' into components and software which would allow China's security agencies to either monitor or manipulate networks. This is vehemently denied by Huawei, which says it has no links to the Chinese government.

Whatever the rights and wrongs of the situation, US legislation and the pressure it has exerted on other governments is having a huge impact on Huawei's sales which dropped by almost 30 percent in 2021 (Hille, 2021). Australia, New Zealand, Canada and Sweden have banned Huawei from their networks completely, while the UK has committed to removing its components from 5G networks by 2027.

However, Huawei continues to exert considerable control on many networks, not just in developing markets where the USA's influence is weaker, but even in countries such as Germany. More than half (59 percent) of Germany's 5G access network products were provided by Huawei at the end of 2022, although the network's core control centre is now supplied by Ericsson (Morris, 2022).

THE IMPLICATIONS OF BANNING HUAWEI FROM 5G NETWORKS

The importance of the US government's decision to ban Huawei from 5G networks cannot be understated. The company was providing the critical infrastructure to power the development of the 'Fourth Industrial Revolution' with all the attendant economic, social and environmental benefit this would bring. Currently there are only three companies which lead the way in 5G technology: Ericsson, Huawei and Nokia. The limited number of players in the market is of concern for buyers of infrastructure and governments alike. It limits choices in terms of technology solutions and could inflate costs. Reducing this triad to just two companies exacerbates these challenges and increases risk of over-reliance on one supplier. It also means the delay of the rollout of new networks (Morris, 2019).

The world is entering a new era of innovation, and 5G technology will play an important role in the facilitation of flows of data which will be generated by such developments as the internet of things (IoT). For example, 5G will be essential for the development of autonomous, connected vehicles, allowing artificial intelligence to assess situations and make decisions many times faster than humans are able to react. Its responsiveness with the cloud (latency) will also enable drone technology and healthcare monitoring systems (amongst many others), whilst it will be able to support at least 1 million devices per square kilometre. It requires very little energy too, which means that devices can be connected for years without continued human maintenance. This has enormous potential for monitoring and managing extended supply chain networks, as it allows for IoT sensors to be distributed across the entire network, reporting constantly on state and location. Detailed visibility at this level provides early warning of any problems, enabling supply chains to continue to flow smoothly and also impedes theft and counterfeiting.

However, the requirements of the technology mean a very dense network of base stations and for mobile communications, a new generation of smartphones. In most countries, investment is just beginning and the rollout has been focused on parts of large cities rather than attempting to build-out national networks. The expectation according to Nokia, however, is that 5G will reach 45 percent of world population coverage by 2024 (Pätzold, 2019). Those countries which choose to exclude Huawei will be considerably competitively disadvantaged.

HOW REAL IS THE THREAT?

In 2017, the Chinese government passed a 'National Intelligence Law' which compelled Chinese companies to 'support, cooperate with and collaborate in national intelligence work'

(BBC, 2019). This resulted in the US, Australia and New Zealand blocking local communication companies from using Huawei components, with Canada and the UK (part of the Five Eyes security cooperation) following suit shortly after.

Security efforts are focused both at 'the edge' of networks (the smartphones) and at the 'core' (the network infrastructure). With far more suppliers and third parties being involved in the development and maintenance of infrastructure, there are more opportunities for these networks to be subverted. This could involve the re-routing of data for malign purposes – either criminal or, as the US fears, geo-political. As this infrastructure is the principal mechanism for monitoring and managing global trade flows, any inherent capability that could be exploited for malign intent has huge implications.

However, according to some, tampering by Chinese agents in Huawei's manufacturing process would be difficult. Many of the suppliers it uses – especially in the semiconductor sector – are based outside of China in countries which have more loyalty to the US than China, for example, Taiwan. It is also noted that a supplier may not have malicious intent in leaving open a 'backdoor' to hackers, which is more likely to be caused by poor software development processes. It is not just the infrastructure equipment providers which represent a risk: the operators themselves could create vulnerability by failing to properly design, secure, monitor and maintain their 5G networks.

HUAWEI'S SUPPLY CHAIN TRANSFORMATION

Although Huawei had been in the US administration's sights for some years, regulations were quickly ratcheted up after 2018, culminating in the ban of the sale of intellectual property (IP) by US companies to Huawei and its affiliates. This escalation came about, according to officials, as Huawei had been successfully 'de-Americanizing' its supply chain. That is to say, it had been replacing US suppliers with Asian alternatives in order to access US-made technologies. The tighter regulations ruled that no supplier to Huawei should use US components or software (IP) in its products. As a result, if Huawei turned to another non-US supplier which used US software and IP to design its products, that supplier would be banned from selling goods into the US market unless it was granted a special licence by the US authorities. Another consequence of this is that as Huawei will be forced to use smaller Chinese suppliers that may be commercially invisible outside of China, it will become impossible to monitor the technology they are providing. Of perhaps most relevance to Huawei's 5G business, the latest regulations require that any company wanting to produce semiconductor chips using US-made tools (such as those produced by Applied Materials or Lam Research) would require such a licence.

According to one report, prior to the ban Huawei sourced $11 billion worth of goods from US suppliers in 2018 (Duchatel, 2018). These included:

- Broadcom
- Qualcomm
- Seagate
- Intel
- Texas Instruments
- Skyworks Solutions (communication semiconductors)
- Qorvo (communication semiconductors)
- Micron (dynamic random access memory (DRAM))
- Synopsis (chip software)
- Corning (cover glass).

In terms of software, Huawei's smartphone used, until recently, Google's Android. However, it has now developed its own operating system, HarmonyOS, which since 2021 has been rolled out across its product range. In terms of components, 60 percent of the value of Huawei's latest smartphones is now sourced from China, compared with just 30 percent a year earlier. This includes chips made by HiSilicon, the display made by BOE Technology and the battery made by Sunwoda Electronic (Matsumoto et al, 2021).

The main non-US companies which still make key components for its smartphone are:

- Sony, Japan (camera)
- SK hynix, Korea (memory)
- Kyocera, Korea (oscillator)
- Asahi Kasei, Japan (digital compass).

German chipmaker, Infineon, and UK designer, ARM Holdings no longer provide technology. Some US chips are still being used, but only from existing stocks which are now running down.

Compared with smartphones, it will be more difficult for Huawei to replace its chip supplies for its 5G infrastructure business. The type of chips which enable 5G base stations to function will be badly affected by the new US sanctions and this will mean that once Huawei has used up its stockpiles, it could potentially become unable to operate in this market, without making other arrangements.

In terms of its 5G base station infrastructure plans, its main challenge will be access to Field Programmable Gate Arrays, a technology provided by only US companies, Xilinx and Altera. It is developing new technology to replace this, but in partnership with Taiwan Semiconductor. When the new regulations bite, the Taiwanese company may not want or be able to supply products to Huawei.

In terms of assembly, Huawei uses a number of contract manufacturers as well as its own facility in Dongguan, China. These include:

- *Flex (Zhuhai, China) – contract ended*
- FIH Mobile (a subsidiary of Taiwan's Foxconn)
- BYD (China)
- Huaqin Communication Technology (China)
- Wingtech (China).

Following the original blacklisting in May 2019, Singapore-based/US-listed Flex (Huawei's largest smartphone assembler with business amounting to ¥2.5 billion) paused its dedicated Changsha, Hunan assembly lines whilst it undertook an audit to assess compliance with the order. Not all Huawei's lines are affected by the US regulations, providing a certain amount of confusion at the time over what suppliers could and could not do. Although it started work again, several months later the two companies ended their partnership when Huawei failed to make commitments to Flex related to compliance. The business was taken over by Chinese rival, BYD (CGTN, 2019).

Huawei's efforts to build stockpiles of components ahead of a full ban is evidenced by its days of inventory (DSI) as shown in Figure 5.1. This metric rose from 69.6 in 2018 to 89.8 in 2019. This would suggest, as also referenced anecdotally, that Huawei built up stocks which allowed it to keep manufacturing until new sourcing arrangements were put in place.

Despite all this, it is still managing to win deals especially in developing markets. Following its ban from the US, Huawei still claims to have built 140 5G networks in 59 countries including in Kenya, Cambodia, UAE, Malaysia, Qatar and Bahrain

Figure 5.1 Huawei: days of inventory.

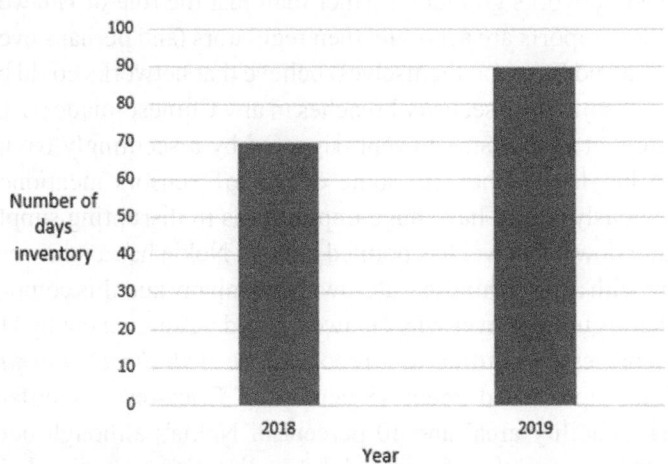

Source: Manners-Bell (2021).

(S&P Global, 2022). This would suggest that it is increasingly confident that it will be able to successfully de-Americanize its supply chains both of product and IP.

NOKIA AND ERICSSON: DUAL SUPPLY CHAINS

The two largest players in the 5G market apart from Huawei are European telecoms infrastructure providers Finland-based Nokia and Swedish Ericsson. Both companies will be set to benefit from Huawei's exclusion from the development of 5G networks.

There have been reports that both companies are considering the option of splitting their supply chains in order to calm fears of US and European regulators over the use of Chinese-made components (Isaac, 2019). It is believed that Nokia has been looking at an exclusively European supply chain, whilst Ericsson is reviewing the possibility of Western and Eastern hemisphere supply chains. At the same time as helping to allay fears in Brussels, London and Washington, establishing an Asian or largely Chinese supply chain to serve China would help avoid any countermeasures in a tit-for-tat trade war.

This suggests that Western fears about Chinese intervention in 5G networks go much further than just the role of Huawei. If these reports are accurate, then regulators (and perhaps even Nokia and Ericsson themselves) believe that networks could be compromised by security breaches in any Chinese-made parts. Note that even a small event triggered by a seemingly trivial and low-level action (in some of the IoT sensors mentioned previously) could have huge implications in disrupting supply chain flows. Huawei has pointed out that Nokia has a joint venture with a part Chinese state-owned company and this complicates arguments over why Huawei should be singled out by US authorities. According to a report in the *Wall Street Journal*, China represented about 45 percent of Ericsson's 'manufacturing-facility area' and 10 percent of Nokia's although both companies say they have a globally diversified supply chain footprint (Woo and Volz, 2019).

If all Chinese components were excluded from telecom networks, this would have a seismic impact on the development of the infrastructure underpinning the growth of Western economies.

THE FUTURE FOR HIGH-TECH SUPPLY CHAINS

Before the ban, Huawei's supply chain was very similar to many other consumer electronics companies. It sourced components from all over the world which were then assembled at its plants in China before being shipped back to the rest of the world.

Its supply chain has transformed from 'global' to 'indigenized' within a very short period. It is evident that as the US puts pressure on its remaining suppliers that its supply chain will rapidly become exclusively Chinese, perhaps with the exception of low value adding technology. The US is still granting licences to companies (such as Taiwan Semiconductor) to work with Chinese manufacturers or even establish operations in the country itself as long as the technology involved is not considered advanced.

Huawei is not the only company which has fallen foul of US policy. Similar steps have been taken to exclude ZTE, a

Figure 5.2 Huawei's past and future 'indigenized' supply chain.

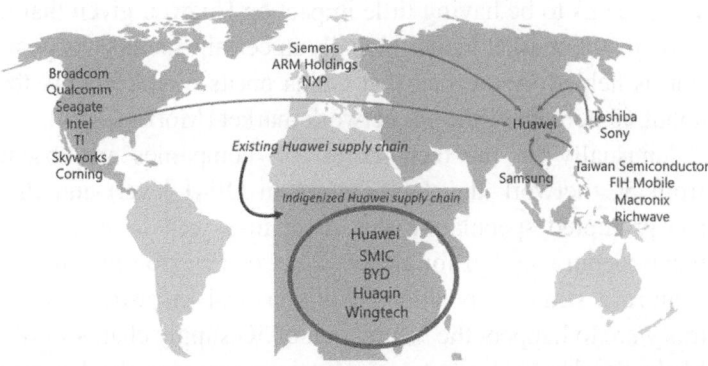

Source: Author.

Chinese telecommunications equipment and systems company, which was found to be supplying North Korea and Iran contrary to US sanctions.

Ultimately this policy of supply chain weaponization may well be so effective, in the present US administration's eyes, that it could be rolled out to other Chinese tech companies as part of the present trade war or to increase leverage with China over policy matters, such as Hong Kong.

However, purely in terms of economics and supply chain, its impact will be wholly negative.

- It will deny the rest of the world access to Huawei's market-leading technology.
- It is likely to delay the rollout of 5G networks in many countries.
- It will increase the dependency of mobile network operators on just two main infrastructure equipment suppliers.
- It will increase cost of 5G development.
- It will have an economic impact on the US and international suppliers of components and services to Huawei in terms of profits (and jobs).
- It will encourage Huawei to invest in many technology sectors in China, stimulating further development.

Despite all the bellicose pronouncements from Washington, as yet it seems to be having little impact on Huawei, given that it remains the market leader globally in certain sectors. Its position is helped by the fact that China on its own accounts for about 60 percent of the 5G network market (Morris, 2020).

Unusually for the tech sector, US companies are absent from 5G network development (at an OEM level) and this has prompted speculation that there may well be a government-encouraged bid for either Nokia or Ericsson in order to acquire a strategic position in this critical infrastructure. If this were to happen, the bifurcation of 5G supply chains would likely accelerate. Even worse, tensions between the US and

China could spill over to other parts of the sector. Already, PC manufacturer Lenovo is being seen as a potential security risk.

As already referenced, it is difficult to discriminate between legitimate security fears and neo-protectionism. In some respects, however, this doesn't much matter – the end result could be the same with companies forced to build sub-optimal and costly supply chains which develop on political rather than economic lines.

CONCLUSION

The political pressure which the USA has brought to bear on Huawei since the Trump presidency has forced it to undertake a complete supply chain restructuring. Not only are telecoms providers in the West in the (admittedly long) process of removing Huawei parts from their networks, but US companies are no longer able to provide the company with advanced technologies. As a result Huawei, and other Chinese businesses with links to the government, must look to 'indigenize' their supply chains and rebuild their business models. This will have consequences for the West. Many countries' 5G networks will take years longer to roll out and will be costlier for taxpayers. However, intelligence agencies believe that this is a price worth paying to ensure national security.

REFERENCES

BBC (2019) Huawei: Should we be worried about the Chinese tech giant? BBC. Available from https://www.bbc.co.uk/news/business-46465438

CGTN (2019) Huawei kicks its top phone assembler out of the supply chain, CGTN, Beijing. Available from https://news.cgtn.com/news/2019-07-18/Huawei-kicks-its-top- phone-assembler-out-of-the-supply-chain-Ir4fTFS79S/index.html

Duchatel, M (2018) Huawei's 5G Supply Chain: Taiwan Winning Twice? Institut Montaigne. Available from www.institutmontaigne.org/en/analysis/huaweis-5g-supply- chain-taiwan-winning-twice

Farrell, H and Newman, A (2022) Weaponized Globalization: Huawei and the Emerging Battle over 5G Networks, Global Asia. Available from www.globalasia.org/v14no3/cover/weaponized-globalization-huawei-and-the-emerging-battle-over-5g-networks_ henry-farrellabraham-newman

Hille, K (2021) Huawei revenues fall 30% in 2021 but company is cautiously optimistic, Financial Times. Available from www.ft.com/content/22d89af2-c3e2-479b-8baf- 5e079ff73458

Isaac, A (2019) Nokia and Ericsson plan emergency break-up over trade war and security fears, Daily Telegraph. Available from www.telegraph.co.uk/business/2019/06/08/exclusive-nokia-andericsson-plan-emergency-break-up-trade-war/

Manners-Bell (2021) Weaponizing high-tech supply chains: Huawei and the US Government, Foundation for Future Supply Chain. Available from https://futuresupplychains.org/whitepaper/weaponizing-high-tech-supply-chains-huawei-   and-the-us-government/

Matsumoto, N, Ryugen, H and Kawakami, T (2021) Chinese components double to 60% in new Huawei smartphone, Nikkei Asia. Available from https://asia.nikkei.com/Spotlight/Huawei-crackdown/Chinese-components-double-to-60-in-new-Huawei- smartphone

Morris, I (2019) Vodafone CEO: Huawei Ban Equals Two-Year 5G Delay, LightReading. Available from https://www.lightreading.com/mobile/5g/vodafone-ceo-huawei-ban- equals-two-year-5g-delay/d/d-id/749690

Morris, I (2020) Nokia gives up on 5G radio business in China, LightReading. Available from https://www.lightreading.com/asia/nokia-gives-up-on-5g-radio-business-in- china/d/d-id/759305

Morris, I (2022) German reliance on Huawei has grown in 5G era – report, LightReading. Available from www.lightreading.com/5g/ german-reliance-on-huawei-has-grown-in- 5g-era---report

Pätzold, M (2019) 5G is Going Live in Country After Country, Institute of Electrical and Electronics Engineers. Available from https://ieeexplore.ieee.org/stamp/stamp.jsp?arnumber=8907479

S&P Global (2022) 5G tracker: 79 markets worldwide have commercial services, S&P Global. Available from www.spglobal .com/marketintelligence/en/news-insights/research/5g-tracker-79 -markets-worldwide-have-commercial-services

Woo, S and Volz, D (2019) US considers requiring 5G equipment for domestic use be made outside China, Wall St Journal. Available from www.wsj.com/articles/u-s-considers- requiring -5g-equipment-for-domestic-use-be-made-outside-china -11561313072

6

Securing the Semiconductor Supply Chain

INTRODUCTION

The worldwide shortage of semiconductors experienced over the past three years has caused politicians in Western markets to examine the fragility of the industry's supply chain. In particular, there have been worries about the strategic implications of being reliant on manufacturers in Asia for much of the supply of chips – components which are critical to all industry sectors as well as underpinning the entire green energy transition process. The recent tension between the US and China over the future of Taiwan has led many analysts to weigh the potential consequences of an outbreak of hostilities in the region, given the reliance of the chip industry on Taiwanese manufacturers, especially in terms of the most advanced technologies. This chapter contextualizes the problems faced by global semiconductor supply chains looking at chokepoints in the industry; the leading companies involved; the concentration of risk; prospects for self-sufficiency and recommendations for policy makers.

DEGLOBALIZING CHIP SUPPLY CHAINS

In many respects, developing scenarios in which the US and China go to war is a futile exercise. Such an event would destroy demand in the world's economy, push already fragile markets into a prolonged slump and derail progress towards a green transition. However, there is already a pathway of escalating tension between the two countries which can, and already is, having an impact on trade flows. The visit of the speaker of the US House of Representatives, Nancy Pelosi, to Taiwan in August 2022 prompted China's military to undertake 'live firing' exercises in the waters around the island, disrupting air and shipping lanes. This was a clear signal to the international community that a blockade of Taiwan could be used as a diplomatic and economic lever.

Many politicians in the West believe that a war over Taiwan would be so counterproductive to China in economic terms that even the most bellicose leadership in Beijing would refuse to countenance it. However, whilst this may be true in the short term, China's industrial strategy is focused around reducing its reliance on the rest of the world and this will include developing its own advanced high-tech sector. In terms of semiconductors, this is a course of action being precipitated by US legislation which has placed controls on the export of advanced chip technology to China (the Export Administration Rules or EAR). This, along with the banning of the supply of components to proscribed companies such as Huawei, has led to the development of 'indigenous' chips supply chains on the Chinese mainland, although these are still at a nascent stage. China has set a target of producing 70 percent of its chip supply by 2025 as part of its Made in China 2025 plan costing an estimated $150 billion (Slodkowski, 2022). The more China becomes self-sufficient in critical sectors, the more the rest of the world becomes exposed to asymmetric risk of the economic consequences of a war. Therefore, continued reliance on sourcing 'advanced' technology from a disputed territory just miles off China's coast is being regarded by the West as increasingly untenable.

To address this issue, the United States and the European Union have passed legislation that will encourage investment in semiconductor manufacturing. The UK parliament's Foreign Affairs Select Committee is conducting an inquiry into the country's vulnerability and other countries, such as India, Japan, Taiwan, South Korea and, of course, China have also adopted laws which facilitate and subsidize their own chip industries.

THE SEMICONDUCTOR SUPPLY CHAIN LANDSCAPE

The semiconductor chip value chain is highly complex involving companies from right across the spectrum of industry, both services and manufacturing. Their functions can broadly be categorized as follows:

- research and development (intellectual property)
- electronic design automation (EDA) tools
- chemicals and specialty gases
- silicon wafers
- fabrication equipment
- fabrication/front-end manufacturing facilities/foundries
- back-end manufacturing/assembly testing and packaging

In total in 2021, the market was valued at $528 billion and it is expected to grow to $1.3 trillion by 2029 (*Fortune*, 2022).

As in much of the high-tech electronics sector, a large proportion of the actual production of the chips has been outsourced using a 'fabless' or 'fablite' model. It is estimated that 33 percent of production is undertaken in this way, separating design and marketing from the rest of the process (Brown, 2021). Market leaders include Qualcomm, Nvidia, Broadcom, MediaTek and AMD, which outsource to foundries specializing in making chips for third parties.

Those companies which continue to make the majority of their chips in-house are known as 'integrated device manufacturers' (IDMs) and include Intel (US), Micron (US), NXP (Netherlands), Texas Instruments (US), STMicroelectronics (France/Italy) and Infineon (Germany).

Various geographies tend to dominate different functions within the industry. For example, Research and Development (R&D) is largely funded by US investors; 60 percent of foundries are owned by Taiwanese companies and over half of silicon wafers are produced by Japanese manufacturers. Whilst the US is responsible for 38 percent of the total value chain, this hides the variances and imbalances which exist in specific parts of the supply chain (EC, 2022).

A fair characterization of the industry would be that much of the R&D in the industry is undertaken in the West (companies such as IBM, for example), with the high-value front-end manufacturing taking place in East Asia and lower-value back-end assembly in China.

Presently just over a quarter of the total market value is generated by advanced chips either 10 nanometer (nm) or less in size, but this market will grow quickly, especially at the 5 nm or less level. It should be noted that not all chip manufacturers are equal – only two, Samsung and TSMC are capable of making chips to the highest specification – 3 nm chips were first produced at scale by Samsung in June 2022, with TSMC due to follow on behalf of its customer, Apple (Clarke, 2023). All companies in the industry have been in a race to make smaller, more powerful chips by fitting more transistors on to smaller silicon wafers (nodes). IBM has devised a way of creating a 2 nm chip which will contain 50 billion transistors, achieving 45 percent better performance using 75 percent less energy (Trader, 2021). Although not likely to be in production until 2024/5, the entire Industry 4.0 model – including green energy transition – will be dependent on advanced technologies such as these. Apart from Apple, which uses 5 nm or less in all of their recent devices, Marvell, Huawei and Qualcomm, all began to place orders for this level of performance back in 2020.

Chips are also important to Bitcoin mining systems which are using 5 nm 'application-specific integrated circuits' (ASICs). A number of these are big customers of Taiwanese giant, TSMC, but as many are either Chinese-owned or have heavy Chinese investment, US legislation is starting to have an increasing impact. Major customers include Bitmain and MicroBT, both based in China. Samsung's first customer for 3 nm chips is also reputed to be a Chinese ASIC firm.

The importance of the technology has been recognized by Western governments, especially the US administration, which has been very keen to prevent it falling into Chinese hands. For this reason, as discussed later in the chapter, legislation was passed during the Trump presidency which can prevent the export of chips and/or chipmaking equipment to China without licence. This is aimed at preventing China from copying the technology and developing its own sophisticated capabilities.

It would be wrong, though, to believe that supply chain risk rests completely at the higher end of the market. Lower priced semiconductors such as micro control units (MCUs), priced as low as 50 cents, are used widely in the automotive sector and home appliances. At 28 nm, the technology is regarded as mature and low margin and this has led many foundries to focus on more advanced processes which generate higher profits. However, demand for lower spec chips is expected to treble by 2030 benefiting China's less developed foundry operators, in particular SMIC, which don't have access to advanced extreme ultraviolet lithography (EUV) technologies from the US. The high volumes of chips involved (although not necessarily high value) and their importance to key sectors of the world's economy could mean that China grows to dominate a critical part of the market.

To add to the complexity of the market landscape, semiconductors can also be categorized between memory/data storage and those purposed for 'logic' functions. The former have a shorter lifecycle and are vulnerable to market volatility. The latter, which undertake more complex processing tasks, have higher levels of customization and have longer life cycles. Consequently, different production, supply chain and inventory management strategies are required to effectively meet customer demand. In terms of policy, politicians must

Table 6.1 Chip sectors and major players.

R&D/EDA	Chemicals	Silicon wafers	Equipment	Foundries	Front end (fabless)	Back end
Cadence Design Systems	Shin-Etsu (JP)	Shin-Etsu (JP)	ASML (NL)	TSMC (TW)*	Qualcomm (US)	ASE (TW)
Synopsis	Sumitomo (JP)	Sumco (JP)	Applied Materials (US)	Samsung (KOR)*	Nvidia (US)	Amkor (US)
Mentor Graphics/ Siemens	Mitsui (JP)	GlobalWafers (TW)	Tokyo Electron (JP)	UMC (TW)	Broadcom (US)	JCET (China)
IBM	BASF (DE)	Siltronic (DE)	Lam Research (US)	SMIC (China)	MediaTek (TW)	
	Linde (DE)	SK Siltron (KOR)	KLA Tencor (US)	Global Foundries (US)	AMD (US)	
	Merck	Soitec (FR)	ASM-I (NL)		**Front end (IDM)**	
	Air Liquide (FR)				Intel (US)	
	Taiwan Specialty Chemicals (TW)				Micron (US)	
	Dow/Du Pont (USA)				NXP (NL)	
					Texas Instruments (US)	
					STMicroelectronics (FR/IT)	
					Infineon (DE)	

*capable of manufacturing 4mb nodes or less
Source: Author and EC 2022

be careful when committing taxpayers' money that they don't back the wrong sort of chip manufacturing.

SUPPLY CHAIN FRAGMENTATION

There can be up to 2000 individual steps involved in the production of a semiconductor, involving design, manufacturing and test and packaging. Many of these steps involve significant capital investment and know-how and this has resulted in high levels of fragmentation, the development of virtual networks of supply chain partners and, in some cases, concentration of capabilities and capital (and hence risk) in a small number of specialist companies. Paradoxically, whilst the supply chain may be fragmented, this does not necessarily mean that there are multiple options in terms of supplier choice. Production networks of chips are assortative in nature – that is, there are multiple nodes or 'chokepoints' at various points in the value chain. The supply of materials is also often constrained (such as rare earth metals) or limited to certain geographic locations. In some extreme instances, the industry relies on 'sole suppliers' (only one company exists supplying a service, material or product) which presents obvious risks. In individual supply chains, the use of 'single suppliers' is widespread (alternatives exist but the customer opts to work with just one for commercial reasons). The latter approach carries its own risks, but these can be mitigated if there is visibility and there are plans in place should the supplier face disruption.

As previously mentioned, chip manufacturing is almost uniquely global in nature and no single country (or indeed region) has a complete end-to-end supply chain. It has been estimated that a semiconductor transits an international border 70 times before it reaches its end market (White House, 2021). This exposes the sector to the full spectrum of risk – from political and regulatory, economic and societal to natural disasters and even climate change. As was seen during the

Covid-19 pandemic, it is also vulnerable to 'whiplash' effects as regards customer orders, production volumes and inventory levels. In many respects, it is not surprising that politicians are urgently reviewing how to increase resiliency. However, any policy attempts to change the nature of the market to reduce this risk would have to address the issue of fragmentation and specialization and the underlying financial reasons behind it. The costs of such policy, as we will see, are significant.

SUPPLY CHAIN CHOKEPOINTS

A structural issue affecting the semiconductor industry is the level of specialization required by each and every supplier in terms of:

- manufacturing know-how
- production facilities
- the conditions in which the product is manufactured and shipped and
- knowledge of the regulatory environment (e.g., preventing advanced chips falling into the wrong hands).

Many of the services provided by these companies are impossible to replicate in the short term and, in addition to this, it can take many years for governments to certify operations from a safety and environmental perspective due to the nature of the products being manufactured. This limits the number of companies involved in the supply chain and means that, if there is disruption, it is difficult to source from alternative suppliers.

Geographic concentration

According to a report by Boston Consulting Group (Varas et al, 2021), East Asia (including China) controls 75 percent of manufacturing capacity and supplies many of the critical materials involved in the process, such as silicon wafers and specialty chemicals. The authors note the region's susceptibility to seismic events and geopolitical insecurity. In addition, they highlight that 'advanced semiconductor manufacturing' (10 nm or less) is entirely located in either Taiwan (92 percent) or South Korea (8 percent); both countries, of course, are threatened by their neighbours. TSMC in Taiwan and Samsung in Korea are the only foundries capable of making the most advanced chips, those with nodes below 5 nm.

This also extends to back-end manufacturing. For example, 'ABF substrates', a type of material which connects different components in the chip, are only manufactured in Japan and Taiwan and shortages have in the past led to delays in chip production. At the other end of the supply chain, two US companies, Synopsys and Cadence, account for 80 percent of the market for EDA software. An even more extreme example is Dutch manufacturer ASML which is the world's only provider of EUV lithography equipment.

Upstream sourcing

Whilst much of the political focus has been on the risks associated with concentration in downstream manufacturing, the sourcing of raw materials and chemicals upstream is just as much an issue. For example, there are only two suppliers in the world of high-grade fluoropolymers, an essential material used in the equipment required for the chip manufacturing process: Chemours (US) and Daikin (Japan). Fluoropolymers themselves are made from fluorospar, 60 percent of which is mined in China – a semi-rare earth metal.

The supply of other elements has been in the news recently due to Russia's invasion of Ukraine. The industry is reliant on both countries for the supply of neon and hexafluorobutadiene (C_4F_6), both critical to the manufacturing process, and the recent conflict has resulted in significant shortages. The two major purifiers for Russian and Ukrainian neon are located in Odessa, an area where access is now virtually impossible. According to the Semiconductor Industry Association (SIA) the loss of \$60–100 million in C_4F_6 supplies could lead to the loss of $10–18 billion in lost revenue in the NAND sector alone, potentially constraining production for 2–3 years. Russia also supplies over 40 percent of the world's palladium, another key material (SIA, 2021).

Worryingly for Western administrators, China is by far the largest producer of raw materials for the semiconductor industry accounting for over 40 percent, according to one estimate. The rest of Asia provides 10 percent; Africa, 10 percent; Latin America, 9 percent; and Europe and North America just 4.5 percent and 8 percent respectively (EU, 2022). These figures probably underplay China's role in the supply of the sector's raw materials as the country also has a large influence over the extractive industries in Africa and Latin America as well as parts of Asia through its Belt and Road Initiative (BRI).

The SIA (2021) believes that China is the market leader in the extraction of 9 out of the 17 rare earth metals and a leader in the refining of 14 of them. This is a sobering fact should tensions between the US and China escalate.

SOLE-SOURCE AND SINGLE-SOURCE RISK: TSMC SUPPLY CHAIN EXAMPLE

Tier 1 risk: TSMC is the sole source of advanced logic chip production.

Tier 2 risk: TSMC relies on a sole-source Extreme Ultraviolet Lithography (EUV) tool from ASML (The Netherlands) for its advanced logic production.

Tier 3 risk: ASML relies on its 5000 suppliers, some of whom are single source, to provide components for its EUV machine.

Tier 4 risk: All lithography tools rely on rare gases and specialty materials from single or sole-source suppliers (e.g. Linde, Carl Zeiss, Wonik).

Tier 5 risk: Rare gas suppliers rely on steel factories in Ukraine and China to supply 80 percent or more of rare gases used in the semiconductor industry. Production of these gases is dependent on Air Separation Units (ASUs) at these factories (Semi-Literate, 2021).

DISRUPTIONS TO CHIP SUPPLY CHAINS

The high political profile attained by the semiconductor industry has come about largely as a result of the shortage of chips experienced since the onset of the Covid-19 crisis in 2020. This was caused by the 'whiplash' effect of cancelled orders due to market uncertainty followed by subsequent consumer demand created by stimulus packages, a rush for 'work-from-home' equipment and the development of associated ICT network infrastructure. The demand came at a time when many semiconductor manufacturers were being forced to reduce output due to the impact of Covid-19 regulations and lockdown policies on labour-intensive parts of the production process. This latter issue was especially pronounced for 'back-end' operations including assembly, testing and packaging taking place in multiple countries across East Asia.

Although the chip shortage started to ease in the second half of 2022, the market did not normalize until 2023. Texas Instruments warned investors that Covid-19 lockdowns had affected its ability to deliver orders to certain Chinese customers, leading to a $500 million hit to its second-quarter revenue in 2022. Meanwhile STMicroelectronics was forced to reduce production at its Shenzhen plant, particularly affecting its automotive division. The situation has not been helped by some companies stockpiling more chips than they need as a backstop against future disruption – so-called 'squirreling' behaviour which results in the uneven distribution of constrained stocks. One report asserts that production of up to 3.3 million vehicles had been affected by September 2022 due to a lack of chips (Phillips, 2022).

Supply chain disruption has come about not just from macroeconomic and fiscal volatility. The highly specialist nature of production; the environment in which chips are manufactured and moved and the concentration of capabilities in a very small number of suppliers and geographies has created high levels of fragility. Below are just a few examples of very costly events which have occurred in the recent past:

- In 2019, a deterioration of international relations resulted in the Japanese government imposing export controls on semiconductor materials to Korea, affecting $7 billion of exports a month.
- In February 2019, a faulty batch of chemicals forced TSMC to scrap wafers worth $550 million.
- High levels of pollution around a 3M plant in Belgium forced its closure by the Flemish government. The facility supplies about 80 percent of the specialist coolant, PFAS, to the semiconductor industry and the company warned customers SK hynix, Intel and TSMC that there would be shortages.
- Weather caused power outages at Micron's Hiroshima plant and Renesas' Kawashiri plant in July 2022 in Japan. The effects of such events can be felt for weeks and in these cases resulted in the rejection of products being manufactured at the time of the disruption on grounds of quality.
- Droughts in Taiwan in 2021 caused shortages of freshwater used in the manufacturing process.
- A fire at a power line at STMicroelectronics factory in France led to a suspension of production and this, combined with other shortages, meant that in mid-2022 it had 30–40 percent more orders than capacity (Martin, 2022).

Impact of chip shortages on the automotive supply chain

Shortages of semiconductors have had a material impact on the automotive industry's production capabilities over the past few years and this has highlighted key vulnerabilities in the new structure of the automotive supply chain. The sector has been undergoing a transformation as:

- Vehicles transition from being 'mechanical' to 'electronic' engineering products
- Vehicle manufacturers (VMs) become dependent on semiconductor manufacturers due to changing supply chain power dynamics

- Disruption to the supply of semiconductors becomes a key constraint on the automotive supply chain (Cullen, 2021a)

The shortages had become so bad that at one stage automotive company, Ford, openly speculated about engaging in its own chip manufacturing, emphasizing the changing power relationships within the sector. Mobilizing the capital and capturing the management expertise to create new semiconductor 'fab plants' would be a significant effort for Ford and one that would overshadow its core car-building operation.

Indeed, this aspect of the changing balance of power highlights a key problem. The major chip manufacturers are unwilling to invest in the new production capacity that the VMs need. As mentioned above, the types of advanced chips that are in demand from the ICT, media, energy and related sectors are quite distinct from those required by the automotive sector. Vehicle manufacturers and their suppliers tend to use older designs of semiconductors suited to control comparatively simple mechanical operations such as door-locking systems, cockpit displays or engine management. This is different to the demands of other sectors or, indeed, even the future semiconductor requirement of new-technology vehicles. This will be a difficult problem to overcome, and components or even whole vehicles may have to be redesigned to adapt to available chip designs.

The reasons behind these problems lie in:

- A disruptive, non-evolutionary technological change in the automotive sector, with the parallel emergence of electrical powertrains, electronic dynamic control technology alongside internal combustion engine vehicles. This has created tensions in the supply chain as different technologies are required for the different vehicle types.
- Poor foresight in supply chain management by the vehicle manufacturers. The VMs failed to anticipate how dependent they would become on semiconductors. They also

failed to anticipate how powerless they would be in negotiations with semiconductor producers.

- 'Electronics' has overtaken the 'mechanical' automotive sector. In fact, it might be suggested that the electronics sector has begun to absorb the automotive sector.

The consequences of the chip shortage in the automotive sector have been felt at all levels as well as in the associated logistics industry. For example, Wolfgang Göbel, president of the European finished vehicle logistics (FVL) providers trade association, the ECG, stated that, 'The current microchip crisis threatens the very existence of the logistics industry that moves new cars. Inventories are close to zero, volumes have fallen dramatically, factories are closing without notice, unbalanced flows are destroying efficiency and thus profitability. The result is empty yards, empty workshops, idle and underutilized car transporters, trains and ships'.

Göbel went on to say, '[The] FVL industry is seeing huge variations in volumes at very short notice making capacity planning almost impossible. The problems are not so much in the logistics chains, but mainly in the production lead times and also a bit in the classic bullwhip effect'.

There are longer-term implications of this crisis. One of these will be a shortage of capacity if, as is likely, vehicle manufacturers need to increase production in order to catch up on unfulfilled demand. The other is a structural change. The automotive supply chain is in the process of being transformed, something which will affect all logistics providers whether serving component suppliers, assembly plants or transporting finished vehicles (Cullen, 2021).

GOVERNMENTS PRIORITIZING THE CHIP SECTOR

Attracting foreign direct investment from major semiconductor companies through subsidies and tax breaks has become a key political priority for many governments, both in the West and developing countries. The problem which they face, however, is that the structure of the existing industry has developed over a number of decades – Taiwan made the decision to prioritize chip production in the early 1970s. Transforming or even tweaking this structure will be hugely costly and require a cohesive, integrated effort involving government and business. Developing the necessary ecosystem will demand, *inter alia*:

- establishment of R&D labs
- investment in training and skills
- capital allowances on equipment purchases
- reform of financial markets to allow access to capital
- development of industrial parks
- development of ICT and other infrastructure (including transport, energy and water)
- expansion of incentives to upstream raw materials suppliers.

In terms of direct subsidies, the SIA estimates that Taiwan covers 25–30 percent of the overall cost of foundry ownership over a ten-year period, levels which will have to be matched by competing governments. This explains the huge sums of money which politicians have allocated to their efforts to build-out semiconductor capabilities. Even so, Taiwan's industry is still connected to a global ecosystem and in no way could be called self-sufficient, which, of course, was never its goal.

United States

The US has passed two major pieces of legislation: the CHIPS and Science Act (2022) and the Facilitating American-Built Semiconductors (FABS) Act and has promised $52 billion of federal investment.

According to President Biden, 'The CHIPS and Science Act is exactly what we need to be doing to grow our economy right now. By making more semiconductors in the United States, this bill will increase domestic manufacturing and lower costs for families. And, it will strengthen our national security by making us less dependent on foreign sources of semiconductors' (Biden, 2022).

The provisions of the CHIPS and Science Act will make available:

- $39 billion in incentives including $2 billion for 'legacy' chips used in the automotive and defence sectors
- $13.2 billion for R&D
- $500 million for international information communications technology security and semiconductor supply chain activities.

The FABS Act will provide a 25 percent investment tax credit for capital expenses for manufacturing semiconductors and associated equipment (White House, 2022).

At least four chip manufacturers have announced developments in the US, albeit dependent on the subsidy and tax breaks outlined in the Acts and with additional State subsidies:

- Micron Technologies has broken ground on an advanced memory chip fabrication plant in Idaho as part of $40 billion, ten-year programme of investment in the US.
- Intel has started the development of a $20 billion semiconductor facility in Ohio.
- TSMC has indicated that it will invest $12 billion in a semiconductor campus in Phoenix, Arizona.
- GlobalFoundries is to expand its plant in New York in partnership with Qualcomm.

GlobalFoundries has given no investment figure or timeline, largely as it has prioritized a competing $5.7 billion project in France, collaborating with STMicroelectronics. The French government was quicker off the mark with the promise of subsidies, showing how competitive the market has become (Nellis and Lee, 2022).

As an indication of how important the sector has become in the US public's mind, a survey by IBD/TIPP found that two thirds of respondents (66 percent) said that having a strong semiconductor manufacturing base was either 'very important' (45 percent) or 'somewhat important' (21 percent) to national security (Ralls, 2021). However, the economics of shifting production to the US (or Europe for that matter) are not so positive. According to Forbes, the 10-year cost of a new fab in the US is 30 percent higher than building the same fab in Taiwan or South Korea, and up to 50 percent higher than in China (Wince-Smith, 2021).

Attempts to attract foreign investment have been allied with legislation that can prevent the export of chips and the technology underpinning chip-making equipment. This is covered by the Export Administration Regulations (EAR) administered by the US Bureau of Industry and Security (BIS) which authorizes exports based on grounds of national security, regional stability, missile technology and anti-terrorism.

In August 2022, BIS banned the export of specific semiconductor technologies which it has assessed to have defence capabilities. In a statement, Under Secretary of Commerce for Industry and Security Alan Estevez said,

> Technological advancements that allow technologies like semiconductors and engines to operate faster, more efficiently, longer, and in more severe conditions can be game changers in both the commercial and military context. When we recognize the risks as well as the benefits, and act in concert with our international partners, we can ensure that our shared security objectives are met, innovation is supported, and companies across the globe operate on a level playing field.
>
> *(BIS, 2022)*

One of the technologies specifically sanctioned was 'gate-all-around field-effect transistor' (GAAFET) which is essential to scaling production to 3 nm and below technology nodes. The BIS said that, 'GAAFET technologies enable faster, energy efficient, and more radiation-tolerant integrated circuits that can advance many commercial as well as military applications including defense and communications satellites' (BIS, 2022). Whilst China is not specifically mentioned as the target of the new regulations, it is clear that the controls are designed to place as many barriers in the path of its nascent advanced semiconductor industry as possible. One of the justifications for this policy is that it is impossible to differentiate between commercial and defence uses of advanced chips in China when companies such as Huawei are seen as state actors.

European Union

The European Chips Act makes provision for $46 billion of subsidy with the goal of increasing Europe's market share from 9 percent to 20 percent by 2030.

The European Commission has recognized that Europe has what it calls, '…shortcomings in key chip design and manufacturing competences and facilities'. It is taking steps to ensure its resilience against supply chain disruptions.

To do this it has created a plan with three core pillars:

Pillar 1 The 'Chips for Europe' initiative supporting large-scale technological capacity building and innovation throughout the Union to enable the development and deployment of next-generation semiconductor and quantum technologies.

Pillar 2 A framework to ensure security of supply by targeting the attraction of investments and enhanced production capacities in semiconductor manufacturing, advanced packaging, test and assembly.

Pillar 3 A coordination mechanism between the Member States and the Commission to strengthen collaboration with, and across, Member States for monitoring and crisis response.

According to the European Commission, the legislation will be a success if progress is made towards the following objectives:

- strengthen EU research and technology leadership
- address the skills shortage, attract new talent and support the emergence of a skilled workforce
- reinforce the capacity of Europe for innovation in design, wafer manufacturing and packaging
- establish a framework to increase substantial production capacity by 2030
- develop an in-depth understanding of global semiconductor supply chains and enable the EU to take appropriate measures when necessary (EC, 2022).

Major commitments from semiconductor manufacturers include:

- Intel is to invest €33bn in a new fab plant in Germany; expand its existing factory in Ireland; develop an R&D hub in France as well as production facilities in Italy, Spain and Poland. The company intends to invest €80bn over the next decade. R&D subsidy by national governments will be exempt from European regulations.
- GlobalFoundries along with STMicroelectronics has announced plans for a $5.7 billion factory project in France.
- TSMC has been in talks concerning a new plant in Germany since 2021 but, as yet, no decision has been taken.

Despite the ambitious goal set out by the European Commission, there are many doubts over whether a 20 percent share of the market is achievable. There are also differences of opinion over where subvention money should be directed. Europe's automotive sector requires older, mature chips rather than the advanced sub 3 nm which politicians would like to see manufactured in the region, the latter being more in line with the theme of Industry 4.0.

China

China is making the most determined attempt to become a self-sufficient country in semiconductor supply, announcing plans to invest $1.4 trillion between 2020 and 2025 on advanced technologies, including semiconductors. A report issued by Semiconductor Industry Association (SIA) forecast that China's semiconductor industry could account for 17.4 percent of global sales by 2024, up from 9 percent in 2020, if its current momentum is maintained.

A 2019 study by the Organisation for Economic Co-operation and Development (OECD) found China's four state-backed semiconductor companies received a total of $4.85 billion in below-market loans from China's financial institutions during 2014–2018, accounting for 98 percent of below-market borrowing among the 21 companies identified in the report. These incentives provide a significant cost advantage for firms in China.

However, China is still unable to manufacture chips more advanced than 14 nm node. Increasing US sanctions on Chinese semiconductor exports and imports have also had an effect on the market. For example, the Trump administration mounted an extensive campaign to block the sale of Dutch chip manufacturing technology from ASML to China. These efforts didn't end with the Trump administration and Biden continued sanctions on Semiconductor Manufacturing International Corp (SMIC), blocking US-based companies from selling its advanced technologies over fears that it would use the technology for military purposes. Without access to these technologies, China will be unable to become fully self-sufficient in the immediate future although it can rely on domestic production for certain semiconductor supply.

UK

As a major manufacturing centre and consumer market, the UK has felt the full effects of the semiconductor shortages.

Like Europe and the US, the UK government is keen to maintain its participation in the chip manufacturing industry due to its importance to the economy as well as for national security considerations. The UK's strength lies in its R&D sector, not least the high-tech design company ARM whose processors are used in 25 billion devices worldwide (DCMS, 2022). The UK has very little in the way of actual manufacturing capabilities and that which it has is either focused on older chips or prototypes.

The UK government has put in place the following strategy:

- Ensure the UK has a *reliable* supply of semiconductors – the recent shortage highlighted the fragility of the supply chain and the range of dependencies in other sectors.
- Ensure a *trusted* supply of semiconductors for the UK – as a key underpinning technology, semiconductors hold an important geopolitical position in the tech ecosystem, as well as presenting cybersecurity issues for both sensitive and broad-based applications.
- Protect and grow UK capability, and seize opportunities – whilst the UK does not have cutting-edge silicon manufacturing capabilities, it does have key strengths in semiconductor design, compound semiconductors and in academic research in related fields.

What does not seem to be on the agenda is the actual building of foundries in the way that has been envisaged in mainland Europe. Instead, it wants to see cooperation with the EU and US, recognizing that the present Asian-focused supply chain structures are inherently risky.

However, the UK government also recognizes the imperative to maintain leadership in the sector and the national interest of retaining British-owned companies. In this respect there has been controversy over the acquisition of a leading UK chip company, Newport Wafer Fab (NWF), by Chinese-owned Nexperia and a proposed disposal of ARM currently owned by Japan's Softbank.

The UK government has told Nexperia that it must reduce its stake in NWF using powers vested in it by National Security and Investment Act which came into force in 2022. A private equity company may take ownership (Flaherty, 2022). Meanwhile, discussions over the sale of the important British company, ARM, to US company Nvidia foundered when the UK competition authority stepped in. There were also talks about a potential listing on the UK and US stock exchanges, although once more intervention by the government seems to have ruled out this option (Lewis et al, 2022).

Rest of the world

The Indian government is also keen to achieve chip 'self-sufficiency' through a subsidy of $30 billion which is designed to create an ecosystem which will make the country a global hub for the technology.

Japan has promised $4.42 billion to ensure the safety and reliability of its advanced technology sector and to increase cybersecurity. It believes that the concentration of production in Taiwan resulting from the market dominance of TSMC must be mitigated by developing more of its own capabilities. As quoted in the *Financial Times*, 'It is unsafe if TSMC is only in Taiwan; you have to spread things out a little more', according to a Japanese official. 'This is to counter the risk of a Taiwan war [with China]. That risk is very real' (Hille, 2021).

Other countries which have already achieved leadership in the sector are also investing heavily or developing support packages which will help them maintain their position. South Korea is aiming at attracting $450 billion in private investment by 2030 and Taiwan is offering companies a range of tax credits.

IS SELF-SUFFICIENCY IN CHIP MANUFACTURING FEASIBLE?

The semiconductor manufacturing sector is, in many ways, the embodiment of globalization. It relies on a massive international coordination of processes, data, finance and logistics flows with very little vertical integration. This provides many challenges for politicians who would like to exert more control over an industry which has become so critical to the world's economic, societal and technological development.

- Even economies as large as the US and China will not be able to replicate the complex, global chip supply chains on a national basis.
- Encouraging and facilitating market-leading companies to build downstream fab plants will be hugely costly. They take a long time to build and market conditions may not be as attractive in the future as they are now. This may require years of state subsidy.

The founder and former chairman of TSMC, Morris Chang, commented, 'If you want to re-establish a complete semiconductor supply chain in the US, you will not find it as a possible task. Even after you spend hundreds of billions of dollars, you will still find the supply chain to be incomplete, and you will find that it will be very high cost, much higher cost than what you currently have' (Ting Fang and Li, 2022).

According to the report by Boston Consulting Group (Varas et al, 2021) establishing self-sufficient local semiconductor supply chains would cost $1 trillion in investment and result in an increase in prices of between 35 percent to 65 percent. However, the authors certainly believe that investment and support by governments could be worthwhile to mitigate risk. They state that, '…a $50 billion incentive program could enable the construction of 19 advanced fabs for logic, memory, and analog semiconductors over the next ten years, doubling the number expected if no action is taken'. This would increase resilience by maintaining a 'viable manufacturing capacity' to meet demand in sectors of national importance to the US.

It is also unclear whether 'deglobalization' of the semiconductor industry is even possible given the complex, interwoven networks of product, data and process flows. Certainly, the concept of 'ally sourcing' – the bifurcation of supply chains along political lines – is problematic. Many countries, especially East Asian, will not want to cut off links with China which is their largest market; nor will they want to upset the US where most R&D is conducted. South Korea, for example, in August 2022 entered into a mutual economic collaboration agreement with China known as the 'Collaborative Supply Chain Council' designed to address any potential disruption to chip supply chains. Forty percent of Korean semiconductor exports are destined for China, and Samsung produces 40 percent of its NAND flash memory in Xian, China (Foster, 2022). At the same time, South Korea is also part of the 'Chip 4' group led by the US government which, as well as these two countries, includes Japan and Taiwan. The US policy objective of the group is to choke off China's nascent chip industry, at least at the high end of the market, and the US CHIPS Act backs up this objective through tax breaks and subsidies.

However, there are other worries resulting from the complexities of both supply chains and commercial relationships. Some of the Asian members of 'Chip 4' fear that the initiative will lead to US companies gaining access to their intellectual property: many of the companies in the industry are customers of each other as well as collaborators, but they also compete, e.g., TSMC and Intel.

The bottom line is that China is the world's largest importer of both semiconductors and manufacturing equipment. All companies in the sector – including US – have a lot to lose by attempting to cut China out of their supply chains.

Other experts believe that measures such as the US Export Administration Regulations will be counterproductive. By being too proscriptive in what non-US companies can export to China, there is the risk that a completely new ecosystem of Chinese, East Asian and even European chip producers will develop using non-US technologies. Presently many companies, such as TSMC, may believe this is not worth the investment or the risk given that a large proportion of the market has so far been unaffected by the controls. However, if tightening US regulations start to impact substantially on revenues and profits, many industry leaders will be forced to look at new strategies to maintain their position in the Chinese market. This truly would lead to the bifurcation of supply chains, increasing costs whilst at the same time failing to achieve the US policy objectives (Fuller, 2022).

HALTING CHINA'S AMBITIONS

The Covid-19 pandemic, the subsequent disruption to production plans and orders as well as supply disruption as a result of lockdowns has put chip shortages high up on the list of many countries' political priorities. The US, EU and UK have all published policy papers which place the assurance of chip supplies at the heart of their industrial strategies.

However, as this chapter has discussed, the semiconductor industry has developed, from its very inception, as a globalized, virtual network of specialist, capital-intensive companies each focused on a small number of the many different processes involved in the design and manufacture of a technologically advanced product. Despite political rhetoric, the complexity of these supply chains would be almost impossible to replicate on an intra-country basis in even the largest markets such as US and China. The capital and expertise required to build new capabilities would be beyond even the deepest budgets and the volatility of parts of the market would make bets on specific technologies very risky.

The response of Western nations has also been influenced by the growing power of China on the world stage and its threat to Asian neighbours, not least Taiwan. As has been noted, one of the biggest concentration of risks in the semiconductor industry lies in this disputed territory which is the home market and manufacturing base for the world's most advanced semiconductor company, TSMC. As the Japanese official referenced earlier in the chapter makes clear, the threat of an invasion of the island has to be taken seriously. Economically it could be argued that China would be the biggest loser from such an action due to the subsequent crash in the world's economy and the massive impact it would have on its own high-tech industry. However, the political kudos that reunification would give the Chinese president Xi Jinping may outweigh the economic catastrophe it would precipitate, making such action at the very least a possibility.

China's increasingly aggressive stance on the world stage, both economically and militarily, has reinforced the view, especially in the US, that flows of intellectual capital and advanced technologies must be constrained to slow the development of its capabilities. This will necessarily place barriers in the way of frictionless trade which facilitates the smooth running of the sector inevitably leading to the fracture of the existing global systems.

The imperatives of a political response to China's ambitions and the need to assure supplies of semiconductors by reducing risk have led to a chip-subsidy 'arms race' which could transform supply chains. Even though most politicians recognize that the development of an end-to-end supply chain would be impossible to create, many believe that crucial capabilities can be developed which will reduce the concentration of risk at particular stages of the manufacturing process. Many countries have focused on the foundry and back-end production elements, but this ignores other threats such as control of the extraction of many of the raw materials required, much of which are located in China or mined by Chinese companies. Therefore, it will be essential to adopt a trusted partner approach along with any reshoring of production capabilities, in other words 'ally sourcing'. This is easier said than done. Even staunch allies such as Taiwan, Japan and South Korea in the Chip 4 alliance, have competing priorities and will not be happy to give up a large and lucrative market as China if the US insists on 'exclusivity'.

CONCLUSION

In summary, it will be impossible even for economic giants such as the US or China to de-globalize semiconductor supply chains completely. However, systemic weakness of parts of the supply chain must be addressed if future supply is to be assured. There is the temptation to focus on the downstream manufacturing capacity – and this is indeed a key 'chokepoint' given that such a large proportion of the advanced chip market is accounted for by just two countries – Taiwan and South Korea – both of which face existential risks. However, sole sourcing occurs throughout the supply chain, not least in terms of key raw materials or chemicals, and disruption to their supply can result in long-lasting production constraints. Governments can play a role in identifying weaknesses and support investment by the commercial sector in plugging strategic gaps or optionalizing the supplier base.

The semiconductor arms race which chip shortages and security fears have precipitated is unlikely to end well. It is highly probable that the additional manufacturing capacity which is being developed will end in an over-supply, causing prices to plummet and threatening to make production unsustainable in a market which is already facing years of uncertainty. Increasing partnerships with allies in Eastern Asia based on commercial realities rather than political doctrine would create a more sustainable model given that Western financial budgets will inevitably be constrained. Perhaps counter-intuitively, further integrating Taiwan's existing capacity into global supply chains would strengthen what is called its 'silicon shield', increasing rather than diminishing the industry's resilience.

REFERENCES

Biden, J (2022) Statement from President Biden on House passage of CHIPS and Science Act to lower costs, create good-pay jobs and strengthen our national security, White House. Available from www.whitehouse.gov/briefing-room/statements-releases /2022/ 07/28/statement-from-president-biden-on-house-passage -of-chips-and-science-act-to- lower-costs-create-good-pay-jobs -and-strengthen-our-national-security/

BIS (2022) Commerce Implements New Multilateral Controls on Advanced Semiconductor and Gas Turbine Engine Technologies, Bureau of Industry and Security. Available from www.bis.doc .gov/index.php/documents/about-bis/newsroom/press-releases /3116- 2022-08-12-bis-press-release-wa-2021-1758-technologies -controls-rule/file

Brown, P (2021) Fabless vendors market share climbs to 33% of chip market in 2020, Electronics360. Available from https:// electronics360.globalspec.com/article/16660/fabless-vendors -market-share-climbs-to-33-of-chip-market-in-2020

Clarke, P (2023) TSMC catches Samsung, starts 3nm chip production, EE News. Available from www.eenewseurope.com/en/tsmc -catches-samsung-starts-3nm-chip-production

Cullen, T (2021) Whilst others boom, automotive logistics suffers, Logistics Briefing. Available from www.ti-insight.com/briefs/ whilst-others-boom-automotive-logistics- suffers/

Cullen, T (2021a) The Automotive Supply Chain, Transport Intelligence, London.

DCMS (2022) Written Evidence from the Department For Digital, Culture, Media and Sport to the Business, Energy And Industrial Strategy Select Committee's inquiry, 'The semiconductor industry in the UK', UK Parliament, London.

EC (2022) A Chips Act for Europe, European Commission, Brussels.

EU (2022) Strengthening EU chip capabilities, European Parliament Research Service, Brussels.

Flaherty, N (2022) UK to force Nexperia to sell Newport wafer fab stake, eeNews. Available from www.eenewseurope.com/en/uk-to -force-nexperia-to-sell-newport- wafer-fab-stake-says-report/

Fortune (2022) Semiconductor market size, Fortune Business Insights. Available from www.fortunebusinessinsights.com/ semiconductor-market-102365

Foster, S (2022) S Korea seeks neutral ground in US–China chip war, Asia Times. Available from https://asiatimes.com/2022/09/s -korea-seeks-neutral-ground-in-us- china-chip-war/

Fuller, D (2022) US controls on China chip tech will crack if tightened too far, Nikkei Asia. Available from https://asia.nikkei .com/Opinion/U.S.-controls-on-China-chip-   tech-will-crack-if -tightened-too-far

Hille, K (2021) TSMC: how a Taiwanese chipmaker became a linchpin of the global economy, Financial Times. Available from www.ft.com/content/05206915-fd73-4a3a- 92a5-6760ce965bd9

Lewis, L, Inagaki, K and Jung-a, S (2022) SoftBank to meet Samsung to explore Arm 'strategic alliance', Financial Times. Available from www.ft.com/content/3b8b11b1- 80f3-4c4e-9bb2 -19e7d308de2c

Martin, D (2022) Semiconductor firms: China lockdowns play havoc with supply and demand, The Register. Available from https:// www.theregister.com/2022/04/28/semiconductor_firms_china _lockdowns_mess/

Nellis, S and Lee, J (2022) GlobalFoundries CEO: New York chip factory likely delayed if US subsidy bill fails, Reuters. Available from www.reuters.com/technology/globalfoundries- ceo-new-york -chip-factory-likely-delayed-if-us-subsidy-bill-2022-07-19/

Phillips, W (2022) Ford braces for $1bn hit from soaring supplier costs and parts shortages, Supply Management. Available from www .cips.org/supply-management/news/2022/september/ford-braces -for-1bn-hit-from-soaring-supplier-costs-and-parts-shortages/

Ralls, A (2021) When will the semiconductor shortage crisis abate? Logistics Briefing. Available from https://futuresupplychains.org/ semiconductor-shortage-crisis/

SIA (2021) Written Comments from the Semiconductor Industry Association Before the Bureau of Industry and Security, Office of Technology Evaluation, US submitted April 5, 2021, Department of Commerce.

Semi-Literate (2021) From TSMC to tungsten. Available from https://semiliterate.substack.   com/p/from-tsmc-to-tungsten -semiconductor

Slodkowski, A (2022) Chip supplier says China will struggle to develop advanced technology, Financial Times. Available from www.ft.com/content/a3e2c685-2f1f-46cf- 892b-c44cdda88919

Ting Fang, C and Li, L (2022) The resilience myth: fatal flaws in the push to secure chip supply chains, Financial Times, August 4, 2022, London

Trader, T (2021) IBM research debuts 2nm test chip with 50 billion transistors, HPC Wire. Available from www.hpcwire.com/2021 /05/06/ibm-research-debuts-2nm-test-chip-   with-50-billion -transistors/

Varas, A et al (2021) Strengthening the Global Semiconductor Supply Chain in an Uncertain Era, Boston Consulting Group, US. Available from www.bcg.com/publications/2021/strengthening -the-global-semiconductor-supply-chain

White House (2021) Building Resilient Supply Chains, Revitalizing American Manufacturing, and Fostering Broad-Based Growth, The White House. Available from www.whitehouse.gov/wp-content/ uploads/2021/06/100-day-supply-chain-review- report.pdf

White House (2022) CHIPS and Science Act Will Lower Costs, Create Jobs, Strengthen Supply Chains, and Counter China, The White House. Available from www.whitehouse. gov/briefing -room/statements-releases/2022/08/09/fact-sheet-chips-and -science-act-   will-lower-costs-create-jobs-strengthen-supply -chains-and-counter-china/

Wince-Smith, D (2021) America's lack of chips is more than a blip, Forbes. Available from www.forbes.com/sites/deborahwince -smith/2021/06/29/americas-lack-of-chips- is-more-than-a-blip/

7

The Influence of Energy Policy on Globalization

INTRODUCTION

Since their discovery, oil and, in more recent times, natural gas have played a critical role in the economic, political and social development of the world. Whilst bringing great wealth, they have also been the cause of huge instability. Those countries or regions which lack these natural resources, including most of Europe, have been consistently disadvantaged, always at the mercy of the markets, the energy exporters, or both. The war in Ukraine has once again demonstrated this uncomfortable state of affairs. However, the present energy shock is just the latest in a long line of similar crises which have occurred since World War II.

The localized nature of oil and natural gas deposits has a profound effect on the distribution of supply chains and this effect is only getting more pronounced. Whilst Europe does not have access to cheap energy supplies and must rely on a global market, other regions and countries, such as the Middle East and US, do. China's demand for oil outpaced its own resources in 1993, but it has immense coal deposits which it relies on for electricity generation. It has also benefited from cheap supplies from Russia (as has India) and this will provide a significant advantage as its economy opens back up after the Covid-19 pandemic.

The importance of oil and gas to the location of manufacturing will lead to a re-balancing of economic and political power, not away from the whole of the West but certainly from Europe. As more carbon taxes are applied to 'dirty' energy sources, this trend will only accelerate.

USA BENEFITS FROM SHALE DEPOSITS

The shale gas boom in the mid-2000s has had a significant impact on the US economy and allowed it to enjoy a level of energy independence not experienced since the 1950s. The innovative process of hydraulic fracturing (fracking) enabled it to access huge gas reserves, making it the largest natural gas producer in the world. The glut of cheap gas particularly benefited heavy, energy-intensive sectors, such as chemicals, where energy inputs are relatively more important than in other sectors such as consumer goods. Research shows that for each dollar increase in the price gap between the US and Europe markets, output in chemical production increases by 1.6 percent (Vieira, 2016). Given that at the height of the European energy crisis in 2022 US prices were $8 per BTU compared with $37 per BTU in Europe (October 2022), the offshoring decisions being made by European manufacturers (see next section) can be placed in context. The comparable price of natural gas in Asia at the same time was $23.5 per BTU (Brower, 2022).

Although the energy crisis in Europe is now approaching its end – cheap Russian gas has largely been replaced with alternatives from Norway, Qatar and the USA – the vulnerability of the European market has been completely exposed. It is true that for decades the import of Russian oil, which was comparable to prices in the US, has kept European manufacturing competitive. However, this does not change the fundamental issue that this arrangement placed Europe at a political and ultimately economic disadvantage. By achieving energy independence, the opposite can be said about the US. As Peter Rosenthal, head of US power at consultancy Energy Aspects says, 'For industrial consumers, [the US] is still a better place than the rest of the world' (Brower, 2022).

What does this mean for global supply chains? There is no doubt that cheap energy has been one of the factors behind the reshoring trend discussed in Chapter 10. It has acted as a 'pulling' force which has combined with multiple 'push' forces relating to economic, environmental, ethical and political risk. As we see below, the opposite is the case for Europe and to a lesser extent Asia.

EUROPEAN ENERGY COSTS PROMPT OFFSHORING

The European energy crisis has added an extra layer of complexity to the decisions which manufacturers have to make about their sourcing, production and supply chain management strategies. Whilst the cost of labour has hitherto been a significant – if not *the* significant – factor in deciding whether or not to offshore manufacturing, the present high cost of gas and electricity has caused what might be referred to as a 'second wave' of production relocation from Europe.

German manufacturer, BASF, has been one of the most high-profile companies to announce major changes to its European business. In October 2022, it announced that it would be permanently downsizing its operations in Europe – and specifically in Germany – due in part to a €2.2bn increase in the amount it had to pay in power prices in the first nine months of its financial year. This has impacted heavily on its plant at Ludwigshafen which, according to reports, uses the same volume of natural gas as the whole of Switzerland. According to Berenberg's energy analyst, Stephen Bray, quoted in *Chemistry World* magazine, 'My view is that BASF is considering importing gas-intensive basic chemicals from outside Europe to use for processing in its European sites. Ammonia is a very gas-intensive operation so switching to imports rather than making it itself could produce costs savings' (Burke, 2022). He believes that it will take 2–5 years before gas prices return to a level where European manufacturers become competitive.

In fact, according to the German Chemical Industry Association (VCI) 13 percent of chemical manufacturers have already offshored production, whilst over a third have cut production and 56 percent have reduced planned investments.

The energy crisis is by no means global – and this is having even more of an impact on European companies. Natural gas is plentiful and still cheap in the US (5–7 times lower on the spot market than in Europe at the time of writing) as well as in Asia, where weak demand from China depressed prices. Those chemical companies with a global footprint (such as BASF) are, as a result, re-balancing their production requirements to locations outside of Europe.

These cost disparities have resulted, for the first time ever, in Europe importing more chemicals than it exports, according to the European Chemical Industry Council (CEFIC). Those companies which are not able to switch production overseas find themselves in an existential crisis. As Marco Mensink, CEFIC Director General, commented, 'We are approaching the point of no-return: if no emergency solution to the energy prices is provided to our sector, we are not far off the breaking point. Hundreds of businesses in the chemical sector are already in survival mode and we have started seeing the first closures. We need action now' (CEFIC, 2022).

As mentioned, this new wave of offshoring is being driven not by labour costs but by the search for lower-cost energy supplies. This provides an interesting dynamic in the process and introduces markets such as the USA and Saudi Arabia into the mix, as well, of course, as China.

To illustrate this, at the same time that BASF was informing investors that it would be making major structural changes to its European business, it was heralding a new €10bn chemical plant in Zhanjiang, China. Given the deteriorating relations between the West and China, this is highly significant: it seems that the company prefers to risk the fallout from an evolving political conflict rather than face the consequences of the present economic crisis. Quoted by Reuters, CEO Martin Brudermueller said, 'We have a very, very profitable China business. Half of the world market is there. What kind of a risk does a company run into if it renounces half of the market?' (Burger, 2022).

It has been said over the past few months that Germany (and Europe as a whole) 'sleepwalked' into the present energy crisis by allowing itself to become dependent on supplies of Russian gas. The same observation has been made about the West's dependency on China for manufactured goods. Whilst the European Commission talks about the necessity to create 'strategic autonomy' in Europe (EU, 2022), this vision is being compromised by high energy costs which are making multiple sectors – and especially chemicals – uncompetitive. Whatever the aspirations to create regional rather than global supply chains, for the time being the reality is being driven by economic rather than political imperatives.

CHINA'S SELF-SUFFICIENCY POLICY

China is the world's second largest user of oil behind the USA and the world's largest importer. Since 2000, China's demand for oil has risen about tenfold. As mentioned, the country became a net importer of oil in the early 1990s: in 2019 only about 3.8 million barrels of crude oil per day were extracted domestically out of a total market of just over 15 million barrels per day (BP, 2020). Even before the invasion of Ukraine, Russia was the largest exporter of oil to China through the Eastern Siberian-Pacific Oil (ESPO) pipeline. However, government policy has always been to diversify supply and Saudi Arabia has consistently played a major role in the market. It has also been government policy to boost domestic supply which has remained almost static for the last 20 years. Companies such as state-owned CNOOC are targeting growth in output of 6–8 percent a year by exploiting new finds, for instance in the South China Sea.

The importance which China's government is giving to increasing energy self-sufficiency is being driven partly by the need to stay competitive in the world's markets. This push is part of a seven-year plan, first introduced by China's president Xi Jinping in 2019 as a response to the deepening trade crisis with the USA. If energy prices rise on a global basis, of course, the impact on competitiveness is muted as all countries are affected. However, where markets are more localized, as in the case of natural gas, Chinese manufacturers which use this type of energy have lost competitiveness against companies in the USA and (in sectors such as chemicals) in the Middle East. The impacts on consumer goods sectors will be more marginal but will still add to the pressures changing the supply chain landscape, especially as regards reshoring to the USA.

It is important to note that China's energy mix is still dominated by coal-powered electricity generation which accounts for 56 percent of the country's energy consumption (BP, 2020). Whilst this proportion has fallen from more than 70 percent in the mid-2000s, in absolute terms coal use continues to rise. Coal is critical to the government's policy of energy self-sufficiency – whilst the US has fracking, China has coal. Both energy resources provide these two superpowers with the ability to (largely) determine domestic and international policy without recourse to global markets or the prospect of becoming an economic hostage to fortune. As Xi himself has said, China must, '…hold the energy food bowl in its own hands' (You, 2022). Whilst there will be a pivot towards more renewables in the future, the principle of energy security will remain. There is no political appetite to risk self-sufficiency for quicker de-carbonization as Xi has made clear. 'Energy security is an overall and strategic issue related to the country's economic and social development and is crucial to the prosperity and development of the country, the improvement of people's lives, and the long-term stability of society' (Xi, 2022).

RISING TRANSPORT COSTS

Whilst input energy costs have an influence on the location of production and consequently the characteristics of the derived upstream and downstream transport demand, the reverse is also true. The cost of transport can also affect where production is located. The price of oil is a major component of shipping costs, although as we have seen during the West Coast ports congestion in 2022, not necessarily the most important. In that instance, soaring sea freight rates were driven by high demand and capacity constraints – both in terms of shipping and other transport asset availability and port throughput. However, there have been times in the past 20 years when an oil price shock has prompted major global manufacturers to reconsider their supply chain structures as a result of its impact on the cost of transport.

An example of this was the oil price 'bubble' of 2008 when prices rose from $90 a barrel in January to just under $150 a barrel in July. It is conjectured that this may have been caused by under-production of oil in the previous years as a result of an effort by Saudi Arabia to manipulate the global oil price (Hamilton, 2009). Supply constraints were exacerbated by soaring demand from an over-heating global economy with growth in the Chinese manufacturing sector a particular factor.

Whatever the reasons for the shock, the price caused manufacturers to re-assess the viability of their global supply chain structures. As one senior Unilever executive said in May 2008, 'Oil prices are now $127–130 a barrel. At $150 a barrel, we start thinking about our supply chain network; at $200 a barrel, we really start thinking about our network'. He went on to add, 'Right now, I don't know what the answers are but what I am saying is that we have to start thinking about the sort of things which when oil was $20 a barrel, no one really did. However, at $150 a barrel, these factors start to become important' (Cullen, 2008).

As it turned out, the shock was short lived and followed by a deep recession. In subsequent years, the oil price returned to elevated levels (between $120 and $140 a barrel between 2010 and 2014) followed by a period in a range roughly between $60 and $80 a barrel right up to the volatility caused by the impact of the Covid-19 crisis.

The capricious nature of the price of oil must be a serious factor in the development of resilient supply chains, at least until the de-carbonization of transport which will, in reality, be many years off. Supply chains have developed on the basis of cheap shipping costs which have enabled the consolidation of production and inventory on a regional or global basis. Expensive transport, partly driven by the underlying oil price as well as additional carbon duties and taxes, negate this logic. Even if oil prices fall back to historically lower levels, the fact that such a large proportion of the world's supply of oil rests in the hands of a relatively few, and not necessarily stable, countries means that the risk of disruption will be ever present.

SAUDI ARABIA'S BIG AMBITIONS

Saudi Arabia is in the process of a transformation. Using the wealth it has amassed from oil extraction, it is pivoting towards a lower carbon, higher value-adding economy, leveraging its geographical location as a regional and global logistics hub.

To achieve its ambition of economic diversification, in 2016 the country adopted what it called the 'Saudi Vision 2030' programme. As part of that effort, Saudi Arabia has spent more than $100 billion on infrastructure and related projects intended to position it as a global logistics hub at the crossroads of Asia, Europe and emerging Africa. Its targets include:

- developing 60 logistics zones to support exports, e-commerce and re-exports, in addition to encouraging trade through land ports
- the growth of re-export revenues from 42 billion riyals to 520 billion riyals
- export growth from 185 billion riyals to 507 billion riyals and

- the expansion of the e-commerce sector from 6 percent to 23 percent of retail sales (SPA, 2021).

In October 2022, a further initiative, 'Global Supply Chain Resilience', was launched which included the promise of a SAR 10 billion package of inducements to attract foreign investment of up to SAR 40 billion to the market. According to a statement by the Saudi government,

> The [Covid 19] pandemic, trade disputes and the geopolitical landscape have broken or weakened global supply chains, driving up commodity prices and disrupting production and distribution. This initiative aims to strengthen the position of the Kingdom of Saudi Arabia in the global economy, and to mitigate the impact of global disruptions. The Global Supply Chain Resilience Initiative will leverage the Kingdom's resources, infrastructure and location to bring greater resilience to economies and companies across Europe, the Americas and Asia.
>
> *(SPA, 2022)*

Whilst logistics and transport infrastructure underpin its strategic vision, Saudi's main aim with this latest initiative is to attract five key sectors to the market. These include:

- healthcare and life sciences
- mining and metals
- real estate
- financial services
- agriculture and food processing.

In effect, Saudi is positioning itself as a low-risk, low-cost and low-carbon economy which would enable investors to access a large domestic market as well as reaching regional and global customers through its transport and logistics infrastructure links. Oil will obviously be a major factor in the economy's development for many years to come. But the government wants to increase its level of value add (in a similar way, perhaps, to China) by using this resource to supply indigenous processing industries such as chemicals, pharmaceuticals, plastics and rubber.

In addition to encouraging inward foreign direct investment (FDI), Saudi has invested heavily in the development of strategic 'trade corridors' with other countries. For instance, trade with India is expected to grow threefold by 2030. Whilst exports of crude petroleum will be an important element of this growth (Saudi is looking to invest $100 billion in India's refining, energy and petrochemical industry) it will also target infrastructure and agriculture sectors, supporting its 'Make in India' initiative.

Likewise, the government also intends to develop its relationship with China with trade expected to double by 2030. Its national oil company, Saudi Aramco, already has long-term agreements to supply China's refineries and chemical plants. However, it intends to align its Vision 2030 with the aims of China's Belt and Road Initiative and has signed deals in a range of sectors including logistics and transport, energy, manufacturing, e-commerce and petrochemicals, mining and housing (StanChart, 2022).

There is no doubt that Western markets will continue to be critical to the success of Saudi Arabia's strategic vision. It is still heavily reliant on the price of oil for economic growth and a recession in Europe and the USA will inevitably depress oil revenues. However, in the medium term, emerging economies in Latin America, Africa and of course Asia will become increasingly important for Saudi's economy as their consumption of oil grows. The decarbonizing West will still require an array of petrochemical products, including plastics, chemicals and pharmaceuticals which Saudi will also be able to supply.

In summary, Saudi Arabia has the resources and ambition to become a major regional and global hub over the next decade, becoming a conduit for trade between some of the fastest growing markets in Asia and Africa, as well as serving the rest of the Middle East and parts of Europe. Its large domestic and export market will give it an advantage over other hub ports in the region which focus largely on transshipments. Its manufacturers will benefit from access to low-cost oil and energy although investors should be cognizant of security risks, especially if relations with Iran deteriorate further.

CONCLUSION

It is important to understand the local and regional characteristics of energy markets in order to gain an insight into the landscape and prospects of the associated supply chain industries. The availability and cost of energy is fundamental to the distribution of production locations in many sectors, especially those which are more energy intensive such as chemical manufacturing. For decades, energy volatility has been an underlying cause of economic and fiscal instability especially in Europe which is so reliant on oil and gas imports. The recent energy crisis has prompted many manufacturers, especially in Germany, to reassess their production strategies: exporters will also be hard hit, unable to compete effectively with US, Middle Eastern and Chinese competitors.

The rest of the world is in a different situation. Relatively cheap fracking energy input costs in the US will provide a tailwind to reshoring whilst China's manufacturers have a backstop of cheap coal. Middle Eastern economies, too, have the advantage of access to cheap energy with Saudi Arabia being by far the biggest beneficiary. The country's hydrocarbons as well as investment in renewables is allowing it to position itself as an ideal location for global manufacturing and logistics services, especially in chemicals and other energy-intensive sectors.

REFERENCES

BP (2020) Statistical Review of World Energy, BP. Available from www.bp.com/content/ dam/bp/business-sites/en/global/corporate /pdfs/energy-economics/statistical-review/bp-stats-review-2020 -full-report.pdf

Brower, D (2022) US natural gas prices surge as Europe turns away from Russian energy, Financial Times. Available from www.ft .com/content/eb251839-d556-472c-8bbf- 243dc9aaf09a

Burger, L (2022) BASF seeks 'permanent' cost cuts at European operations, Reuters. Available from https://www.reuters.com/ markets/europe/basf-says-european- operations-need-be-cut-size -permanently-2022-10-26/

Burke, M (2022) European chemicals industry struggling to compete as costs surge, ChemistryWorld, 27 October 2022. Available from https://www.chemistryworld.com/ news/european-chemicals -industry-struggling-to-compete-as-costs-surge/4016444. article

CEFIC (2022) Energy crisis: the EU chemical industry is reaching breaking point, CEFIC. Available from https://cefic.org/media -corner/newsroom/energy-crisis-the-eu- chemical-industry-is -reaching-breaking-point/

Cullen, T (2008) Oil price surge should prompt rethink about supply chain networks, Logistics Briefing. Available from www.ti-insight .com/briefs/14464-2/

EU (2022) EU strategic autonomy 2013-2023: from concept to capacity, European Union. Available from https://www.europarl .europa.eu/thinktank/en/document/EPRS_BRI (2022)733589

Hamilton, J (2009) Causes and consequences of the oil shock of 2007– 08, Brookings Institute. Available from https://www.brookings .edu/wp-content/uploads/2016/07/ 2009a_bpea_hamilton-1.pdf

SPA (2021) Minister of transport and logistics launches the 'Logistics License', Saudi Press Agency. Available from https://www.spa .gov.sa/2305094

SPA (2022) HRH Crown Prince launches 'Global Supply Chain Resilience Initiative' to position Saudi Arabia as a key link in global supply chains, Saudi Press Agency. Available from https:// www.spa.gov.sa/viewstory.php?lang=en&newsid=2394657

StanChart (2022) Future of Trade 2030, Standard Chartered. Available from https://av.sc. com/corp-en/content/docs/Future-of -Trade-2021.pdf?time=1667234942

Vieira, H (2016) Fracking has made US manufacturing more competitive, London School of Economics. Available from https://blogs.lse.ac.uk/businessreview/2016/12/16/fracking-has-made-us-manufacturing-more-competitive/

You, X (2022) What does China's coal push mean for its climate goals? Carbon Brief. Available from www.carbonbrief.org/analysis-what-does-chinas-coal-push-mean-for- its-climate-goals

Xi, J (2022) The rice bowl of energy must be in our own hands, National Energy Administration. Available from http://www.nea.gov.cn/2022-01/07/c_1310413762.htm (translated)

8

Can the West Decouple
from China?

INTRODUCTION

China's dominance of global supply chains has become a major concern for politicians throughout North America, Europe and even Asia. The issue became a focal point of the last US presidential election with President Trump stating, 'We lose billions of dollars and if we didn't do business with them [China] we wouldn't lose billions of dollars. It's called decoupling, so you'll start thinking about it' (Reuters, 2020). However, how feasible is it to disentangle the US and other Western economies from China when it is responsible for so much of the world's manufacturing output?

A report by the Henry Jackson Society (Rogers et al, 2020) concludes that, 'The five powers [US, UK, Australia, Canada and New Zealand] have become so dependent on China for a number of exports that they may not be able to regenerate self-sufficiency across all strategic sectors, even those that underpin existing critical infrastructure'.

This chapter examines the practicalities of decoupling and how easy or difficult it would be for manufacturers and retailers in the West to look for alternatives to Chinese suppliers.

WHY THE NEED FOR 'DECOUPLING'?

There are many reasons why politicians and corporations in the West are increasingly looking to decouple their economies and supply chains from China. As we have seen from earlier chapters, security is one of the main concerns due to alleged links between Chinese manufacturers and the Chinese government. This has raised fears over the possibility that components used in communications networks (especially 5G) could be compromised in some way, providing security vulnerabilities.

It is not just telecommunications. Chinese companies have become integrated into the working of the West's critical infrastructure including energy, health, information technology and transportation. Not only this, much of the technological hardware on which the Fourth Industrial Revolution is based is manufactured in China. This could provide the Chinese government and/or manufacturers with undue influence over the development of associated markets and consequently over the strategic development of competing economies.

However, national security is just one issue. The global shortage of personal protective equipment (PPE) at the start of the Covid-19 crisis, led many to ponder on the wisdom of allowing the concentration of the production of such essential supplies in one country. In fact, in terms of exposure, there are whole industry sectors – such as consumer electronics and pharmaceutical – which have a high degree of dependency on Chinese manufacturers.

Then, of course, there is the issue of Western job losses which President Trump continually highlighted throughout his term in office. His approach to 'levelling the playfield' has been to levy billions of dollars of tariffs on many Chinese imports to the US.

In addition to these specific China-focused concerns, there are the more general inherent risks related to outsourcing production to remote locations. These include issues such as currency volatility, ethics, environmental practices, natural disasters, port strikes, weather conditions, quality control and cargo crime to mention just a few. The Covid-19 crisis exposed the capacity constraints of the air cargo and shipping markets and the interruption to services which subsequently resulted.

Whilst these risks have, in the past, been outweighed by the cheapness of China's labour and transport, there are signs that supply chain managers may be starting to factor in these additional costs.

But is the global economy already too integrated to be decoupled? A significant part of Western manufacturing has been outsourced to China, along with know-how, technology, expertise and, of course, jobs. Production capacity is also a major factor – in many sectors it is not feasible to find alternatives (whether reshored or elsewhere in the world) to the huge workforces which China is able to supply.

This chapter will look at two sectors in more detail: consumer electronics and pharmaceutical. It will review upstream and downstream supply chains identifying vulnerabilities caused by a concentration of production in China at both an industry as well as raw material level.

ASSESSING THE DEPENDENCY OF THE CONSUMER ELECTRONICS SECTOR ON CHINA

As part of the methodology to assess China's influence over critical supply chains it is useful to look at the concentration of certain key export markets and then assess China's dominance within each. By looking at market concentration it is possible to identify which sectors are at risk from lack of market alternatives and then examine the role of Chinese manufacturers/ exporters, government policy and the risk this presents to Western economies.

One way of doing this is to use the Herfindahl-Hirschman Index (HHI) scale of market concentration/fragmentation. This tool is usually employed by regulators to decide whether company mergers and acquisitions should be given the go ahead given their impact on the market, but it also works very well at a country rather than corporate level. The UN Comtrade database can be used to identify the value of exports in any given product category (using HS codes) in total and by country.

Figure 8.1 Consumer electronics market consolidation.

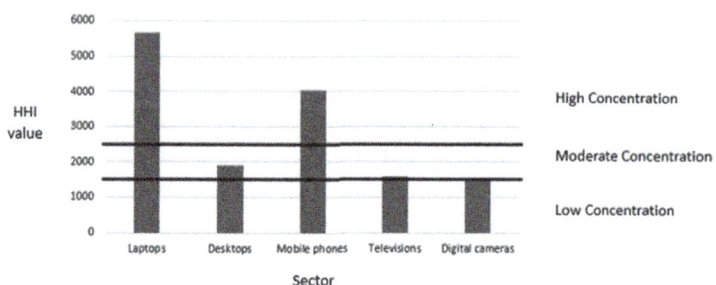

Source: Author.

Taking the consumer electronics export market, it can be seen that, of five key sub-sectors (laptops, desktops, mobile phones, televisions and digital cameras), two are judged to be highly concentrated (a value of >2500).

The next sections look at the supply chains of these two sub-sectors in more detail to identify China's influence.

Laptops

As can be seen from the chart below, the global laptop export market (defined in the HS classification as a portable computer weighing less than 10 kg and having a keyboard, display and CPU) is dominated by Chinese manufacturers which, between them, control a market share of worldwide exports of just under 75 percent. The chart also shows, in terms of alternatives, there are few viable options for buyers looking to source laptops outside of China, especially for the mass consumer market. This dominance has meant that China has developed a strong grip on the production processes, the technologies and the ecosystems needed to manufacture laptops competitively.

The risk identified is not just theoretical. At the start of the Covid-19 crisis, production of laptops was disrupted as the disease spread throughout China causing long delays in shipping. This situation was exacerbated as demand for laptops in the West soared once economies went into lockdown and workers

Figure 8.2 Laptop export market share.

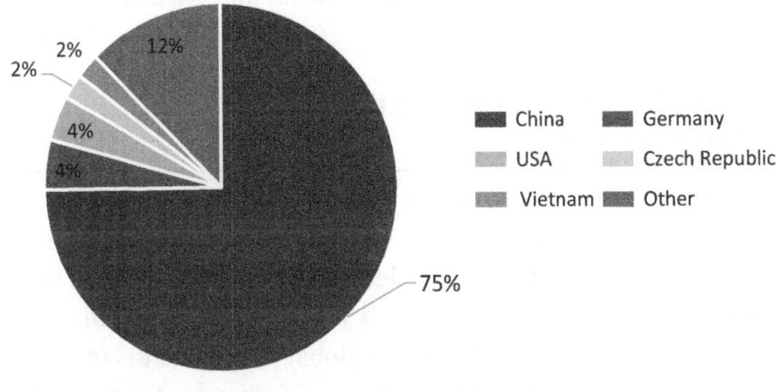

Source: UN Comtrade database 2019.

and children were directed to work from home. This will have had significant but hidden and probably unquantifiable, economic consequences related to price and supply.

Mobile/smartphones

The market is almost as concentrated for the smartphone sector. China accounts for nearly two-thirds of the world's exports of smartphones by value, although there is at least a viable alternative source, Vietnam, which has a market share of over 10 percent. Samsung, for instance, has moved its smartphone factories from China to Vietnam, ceasing production in China entirely in 2019 as it lost market share to local competitors. Google and LG have also relocated much of their production to this new market.

But this is not the whole picture. Although Samsung has closed its own Chinese-based factories, it was revealed by Reuters that it intends to outsource 20 percent of its production to Chinese original design manufacturers (ODMs) such as Wingtech (Yang and Jin, 2019). This could amount to 60 million units a year, of mostly low or mid-range models. LG is also following suit. According to the report, Chinese ODMs can source components from local suppliers 30 percent below the price which companies in Vietnam can obtain. This is because of the economies of scale which ODMs have, already working for giant local companies such as Huawei and Xiaomi.

MOVING UPSTREAM: INTERMEDIATE COMPONENTS

The importance of Chinese component manufacturers is another critical issue in consumer electronics' supply chains. Even if products can be assembled elsewhere, often a large proportion of the parts sourced will inevitably still originate in China. This means that the risk to global supply chains remains – it is just concealed further upstream. Samsung, for example, now sources a proportion of its Galaxy antennas from China as well as smartphone camera lenses. Previously they had been produced in South Korea, but increasing competition in the market forced them to look for cheaper options. It should also be noted that Chinese suppliers have developed the technology to be able to provide these components at the right quality as well as at a lower price. China is now the second largest exporter of camera lenses in the world, behind Japan and ahead of Germany and South Korea.

Figure 8.3 Mobile phone export market share.

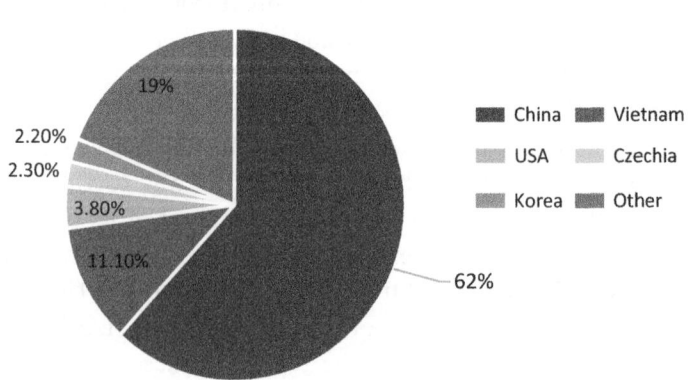

Source: UN Comtrade database 2019.

Indeed, analysis of trade in intermediate electronic products shows that the export market for components for office equipment and computers (HS8473) is highly concentrated, with China the market leader. The export market has an HHI of 2865 (>2500 is defined 'high concentration') and China has a market share of 51 percent. South Korea, the second largest exporter of electronic components in the region, is only a sixth of the size of China.

FURTHER UPSTREAM: RAW MATERIALS

If China's dominance of intermediate and finished consumer electronics products is worrying, their control of the extraction and refining of critical raw materials is even more so. An example of this is lithium, a mineral in high demand due to its use in batteries for laptops, smartphones as well as electric vehicles (EVs).

Although China is the third largest producer of lithium, Chinese companies have invested heavily in mining projects in Australia, Chile and elsewhere to secure the supply of the mineral. In order to achieve its targets related to emissions and the growth of its EV car market, the Chinese government has recognized the importance of securing a diverse supply. Consequently, in addition to investing in companies in the largest lithium-rich countries, it has also targeted secondary markets such as Zimbabwe, Canada and Bolivia. Chinese companies have been encouraged to do so by their government and supported by cheap loans to make acquisitions. This allows these companies to supply China's huge lithium processing industry headed by companies such as Tianqi and Jiangxi Ganfeng. According to analysis by BloombergNEF (BNEF), China controls 80 percent of the world's lithium refining capacity (BNEF, 2020).

This dominance of the upstream lithium supply chain consequently allows China to command the global lithium-ion battery manufacturing market. In 2019, there were 316 gigawatt-hours of global lithium cell manufacturing capacity. Of this, 73 percent is located in China, with the US, the second largest

Figure 8.4 Electronic components, trade value 2019.

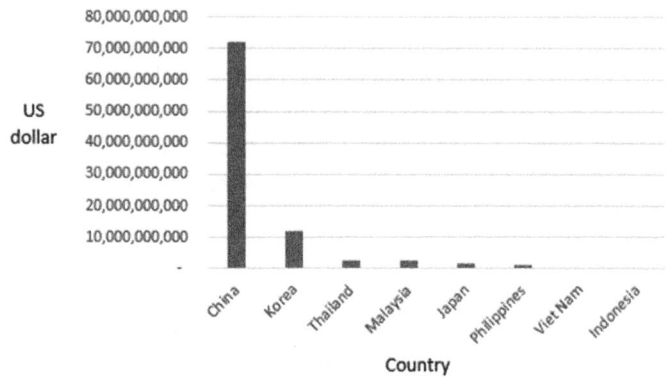

Source: UN Comtrade database 2019.

Table 8.1 The largest producers of lithium

Australia	51,000 tonnes
Chile	16,000 tonnes
China	8000 tonnes
Argentina	6200 tonnes
Zimbabwe	1600 tonnes

Source: NS Energy, 2020

Figure 8.5 Share of lithium battery trade in 2019.

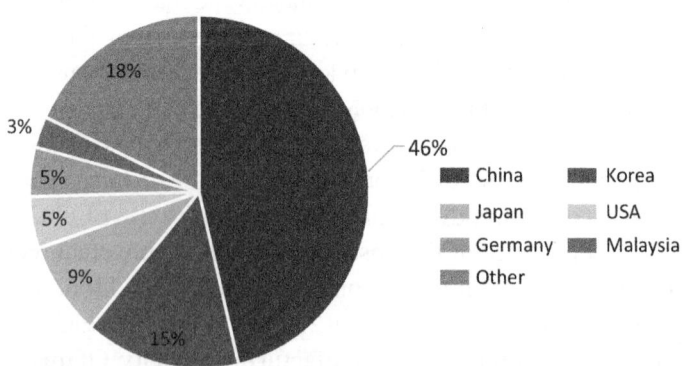

Source: UN Comtrade database 2019.

market, holding a market share of just 12 percent. Whilst much of this capacity is directed to domestic consumption, Chinese manufacturers also dominate the global trade in lithium-ion batteries, as can be seen from the chart below.

According to Kwasi Ampofo, BNEF's lead analyst covering battery raw materials, 'Other countries seeking to be dominant players in the overall value chain may need to support upstream metals mining and refining development'. This really demonstrates that decoupling supply chains from China is not just about switching suppliers to a third country. Rather, if decoupling is to be achieved, it will require strategic investment by companies as well as governments to secure the supply of raw materials. Rivalling the amount which China has spent on pursuing this policy goal will be out of the reach of most countries, with the exception of the US. However, there is little sign that a US alternative to China's Belt and Road initiative will be successful, despite a certain amount of rhetoric.

WHAT INFLUENCE DOES CHINA EXERT ON THE PHARMA SECTOR?

Since 2008, the Chinese government has prioritized investment in the pharma sector as a target high-value industry. Its huge domestic chemical industry ensures the ready supply of chemical compounds to the large number of Chinese pharma manufacturers which have developed in the country. There are accusations that there has been a systematic (and successful) attempt by the Chinese government to dominate the global market by subsidizing the cost of the upstream raw materials as well as encouraging the pharma manufacturers to 'dump' their product on the global market (USCC, 2019). Some have argued that this has changed the whole structure of the world pharma industry, with an increasing and potentially dangerous dependence on China.

At first sight, these fears would seem overblown. The top five pharma companies in the world, so-called 'big pharma',

Figure 8.6 Share of salicylic acid global export trade in 2019.

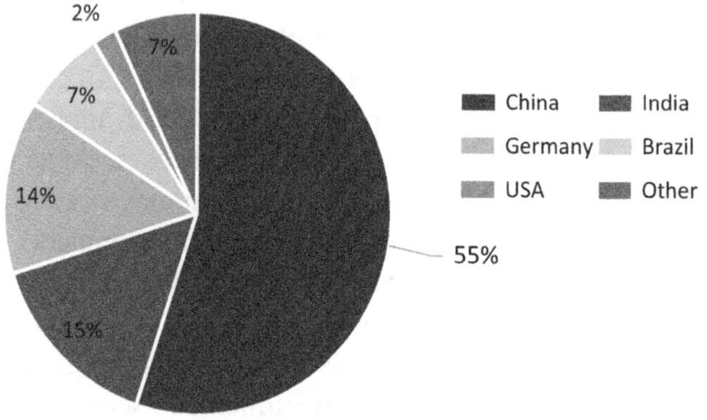

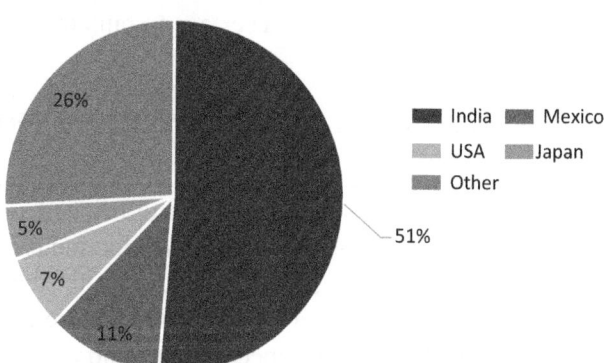

Source: UN Comtrade database 2019.

Figure 8.7 China's key export markets for salicylic acid in 2019.

Source: UN Comtrade database 2019.

are, after all, based in North America and Europe. The largest exporters of drugs by value include Germany, Switzerland, US, Belgium, France and Ireland. However, these companies and countries specialize in higher-value biological drugs rather than the 'generics' – drugs which were previously protected by a patent: these are now manufactured largely in Asia, specifically in China and India. The production of generic drugs relies on large-scale chemical manufacturers to produce the raw materials (the chemical compounds) which are then turned into active pharmaceutical ingredients (APIs)[1]. The APIs are then mixed with excipients (inactive ingredients which act as a medium for the drug such as 'fillers', colourings and preservatives) to formulate a medicine. It is estimated that China accounts for 40 percent of global API production (MHRA, 2017).

If we look at one common API, salicylic acid, better known as aspirin (under HS 291821) it can be seen that China has achieved a position of even greater dominance in this market, accounting for 55 percent of all exports.

Another vulnerability of the API market which was shown up during the Covid-19 crisis is the importance of India as a market for APIs imported from China. The APIs are then processed (combined with excipients) and made into medicines for onward export to the world market. India imposed an export ban on pharmaceuticals during this period which many feared would lead to shortages. The chart above shows the importance of India to China and vice versa using salicylic acid again as an example.

So, over half of the world's supply of aspirin is manufactured in China and over half of this output is channelled through India for formulation into generic medicines.

This clearly reveals the exposure of global pharmaceutical supply chains (at least in certain categories of drugs) to a break down in international relations either between the West and China or, indeed, between India and China, the latter being a particularly significant threat at the moment.

CONCLUSION

The Covid-19 pandemic has been the latest crisis to show up the shortcomings of global supply chains especially those which originate in China. The worldwide shortages of PPE have led to Western governments looking hard at the dependence of their economies on a country which is increasingly being regarded as an unreliable partner. This perception is being reinforced by the role of Huawei in critical infrastructure projects as well as the trade war between the US and China.

As we have seen, examining trade data for certain key sectors – such as consumer electronics and pharmaceuticals – proves that some sectors have become highly exposed to China. To fully understand the level of exposure it is necessary to follow the supply chain all the way upstream to identify who owns or controls the raw materials. In the case of many minerals, including lithium, China not only has its own resources but augments these by controlling extraction in other parts of the world, such as in Australia, Africa and Latin America. 'Owning' the value chain in key sectors has become a strategic goal for the Chinese government.

In the past, there have been concerns over the impact which globalization has had on jobs in the developed world. There have also been worries about the enhanced level of external risk which it creates for the supply chain and logistics industry. Now, however, there are increasing fears related to the security implications of outsourcing the production of intermediate and finished goods to a country which could leverage this power for its own political ends.

NOTE

1 According to the World Health Organization, an API is any substance or combination of substances used in a finished pharmaceutical product (FPP), intended to furnish pharmacological activity or to otherwise have direct effect in the diagnosis, cure, mitigation, treatment or prevention of disease, or to have direct effect in restoring, correcting or modifying physiological functions in human beings.

REFERENCES

BNEF (2020) China dominates the lithium-ion battery supply chain, but Europe is on the rise, Bloomberg NEF. Available from https://about.bnef.com/blog/china-dominates- the-lithium-ion-battery -supply-chain-but-europe-is-on-the-rise/

MHRA (2017) International Strategy, Medicines and Healthcare products Regulatory Agency, UK. Available from https://assets.publishing.service.gov.uk/government/ uploads/system/ uploads/attachment_data/file/609425/Item_10__2017-OB-05_ _International_Strategy.pdf

Reuters (2020) Trump again raises idea of decoupling economy from China, Reuters. Available from https://www.reuters.com/article/ usa-trump-china-idUSKBN25Z08U

Rogers, J, Foxall, A, Henderson, M and Armstrong, S (2020) Breaking The China Supply Chain: How the 'Five Eyes' can Decouple from Strategic Dependency, Henry Jackson Society, London.

NS Energy (2020) Profiling the top six lithium-producing countries in the world, NS Energy. Available from www.nsenergybusiness .com/features/top-lithium-producing- countries/

USCC (2019) United States-China Economic and Security Review Commission, 2019. Available from www.uscc.gov/sites/default/ files/RosemaryGibsonTestimonyUSCCJuly152019.pdf

Yang, H and Jin, H (2019) Made in China: Samsung farms out more phones to fend off rivals, Reuters. Available from www.reuters .com/article/us-samsung-elec-china-focus- idUSKBN1XR0TJ

9

'China Plus' Sourcing Options for Global Manufacturers

INTRODUCTION

A combination of economic and political risk is forcing global manufacturers to look at alternatives to sourcing or making goods in China. As Chapter 8 discussed, options are often limited due to the dominance of Chinese manufacturers in many sectors, not to mention their access to raw materials. In addition, China boasts extensive labour markets, a comprehensive network of supplier ecosystems and has strong transport, energy and ICT infrastructure. However, rising labour costs and the impact of the implementation of US trade tariffs on Chinese exports have provided other countries in the region with the opportunity to benefit from a change in Western sourcing strategies. This chapter examines the prospects of the main alternative markets to China.

WINNERS FROM CHINA PLUS STRATEGIES

'China plus' sourcing strategies have been promoted as a way of reducing the risks of interruption to supply, especially in light of the PPE crisis in 2020. However, if a market is to be considered as a serious alternative to China, it must meet a number of criteria (Figure 9.1) involving decisions based on nine categories:

- political
- sustainability
- workforce

- technology
- supply chain risk
- supplier base
- energy supply
- economy and finance
- logistics.

It takes many years for a country to develop all the necessary attributes which a global manufacturer or retailer will look for when seeking alternative markets to China. Whilst it is critical that the labour costs are lower or at least competitive with those of Chinese suppliers, there are plenty of other 'red lines'. Does a supplier have the requisite experience and expertise? Is the government stable? What are the risks from natural disasters? Are energy, financial and ICT networks sufficiently robust?

Logistics will be a significant factor in market choice for obvious reasons. Not only will road, rail, air and shipping infrastructure need to be high quality and comprehensive but a mature and skilled logistics industry is required to facilitate the

Figure 9.1 'China plus' market choice criteria.

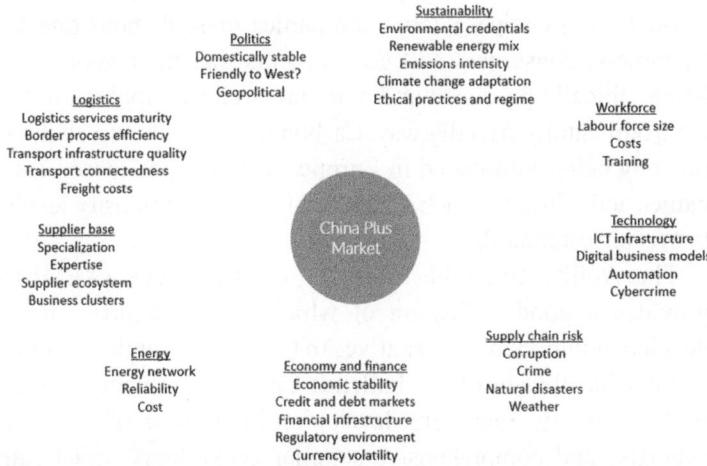

Source: Author.

Table 9.1 Agility Emerging Market Logistics Index international opportunities.

Asian Rank	Global Rank	Country	Rating
1	1	China	9.91
2	2	India	7.65
3	5	Indonesia	6.00
4	6	Thailand	5.98
5	7	Vietnam	5.95
6	8	Malaysia	5.86
7	13	Philippines	5.31
8	23	Sri Lanka	4.73
9	24	Pakistan	4.72
10	33	Cambodia	4.48

Source: Ti Insight (2023)

efficient movement of imports and exports. The number and frequency of shipping calls is important, as are issues such as the number of destinations served and whether transhipment is needed. If the latter, transit times are often protracted and logistics costs higher.

Sustainability will also play an increasingly important role in offshoring choice. Global companies must demonstrate to customers, consumers and governments that their goods are being ethically produced and manufactured by suppliers in an environmentally friendly way. Carbon tax adjustments, such as the levy being introduced in Europe, will penalize those companies and markets which do not reduce carbon intensity levels to Western standards.

The Agility Emerging Market Logistics Index (AEMLI) provides a good indication of which Asian countries have developed into viable alternatives to China. Although no single country has the ability to challenge China's dominant position in the rankings, many are developing high levels of industry expertise and comprehensive supplier ecosystems which can effectively compete in specific sectors and sub-sectors. Using the AEMLI as a guide, the top five markets are reviewed later in the chapter.

'CHINA PLUS' BENEFICIARIES IN THE FASHION SECTOR

Whilst evidence of 're-shoring' is often difficult to find, the results of 'China plus' strategies are more evident. As can be seen from Figure 9.2, over the last 10 years Bangladesh and Vietnam have enjoyed very strong growth rates relating to their clothing and textile exports, especially when compared with China.

The development of alternative manufacturing locations has meant that fashion supply chains have become very much more nuanced than was the case in the past. Although China remains the largest exporter of fashion products, many other 'far-sourcing' options have been developed. This has been a result of rising labour costs, the US–China trade war and a change of political priorities in China which has directed investment to higher value sectors, such as electronics. In addition to these, near-sourcing (South Eastern Europe and North Africa) and mid-sourcing options (African and Latin America) have developed to supply the Western 'fast fashion' sector.

COVID, THE FINAL STRAW?

In 2022, disturbing pictures emerged from China revealing the consequences of President Xi Jinping's zero-tolerance approach to Covid-19. Video footage showed workers at Foxconn's Zhengzhou plant staging a 'break out' by scaling walls in order to avoid being locked down within the factory. Although production could be switched to alternative facilities, up to 10 percent of Apple's global output was likely to have been affected (Kuo and Li, 2022).

Lockdowns of various Chinese cities were ongoing throughout the pandemic, despite restrictions being lifted in most other parts of the world. The policy inflicted considerable

Figure 9.2 Clothing and textiles export growth rates 2008/18.

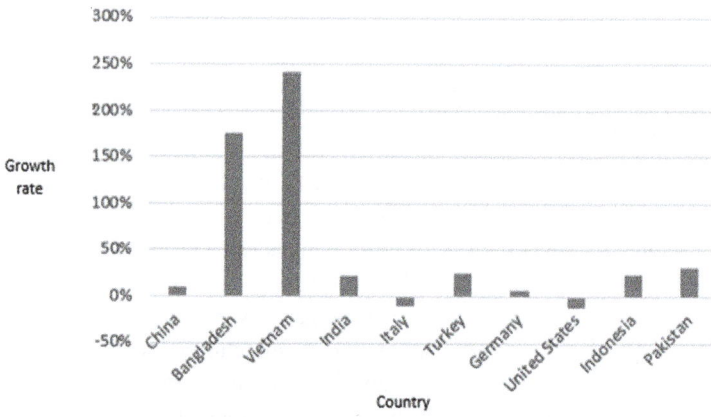

Source: World Bank Trade Data Bank 2019.

pain on the economy contributing to a collapse in US manufacturing orders by 40 percent (LaRocco, 2022). Global fashion brands, such as Nike, faced the double hit that, as well as
closing factories, they were also forced to shutter their retail
outlets for the duration of each lockdown. One estimate suggests that sales dropped by more than 50 percent in affected
areas (Husband, 2022).

There were also consequences for inbound and outbound
logistics. A reduction in trucking capacity in the port of
Shanghai of 45 percent in spring 2022 resulted in 80 percent of
vessels being delayed. Imports were also affected with containers waiting for up to 12 days for collection compared with pre-
lockdown 4–5 days, according to digital forwarding platform,
Freightos (Hollinger et al, 2022).

The lockdowns resulted in significant volatility and uncertainty for global manufacturers and retailers and this in turn
led to increasing levels of inventory, orders being placed earlier
and – most critically for China's economy – the use of suppliers
based in neighbouring countries. Vietnam has been a key beneficiary of this trend: its furniture industry, for example, grew

its share of global exports from 11 percent in 2019 to 17 percent in 2022 at the same time as China's fell from 61 percent to 53 percent (LaRocco, 2022a). It seems that lockdowns for many manufacturers and retailers proved to be the final straw.

However, operating a diversified supply chain is not without its difficulties and it is understandable why many companies have chosen to stay in China. Having multiple suppliers in multiple countries increases complexity and reduces economies of scale and supply chain visibility. Furthermore, having a range of suppliers does not always guarantee that disruption will not occur. During the Covid-19 pandemic, national lockdowns led to the closure of facilities right across Asia.

NEW TRADE AGREEMENTS FACILITATE 'CHINA PLUS' STRATEGIES

As supply chains diversify throughout Asia, the development of trade deals takes on renewed importance. The Comprehensive and Progressive Agreement for Trans-Pacific Partnership (CPTPP) is one such agreement that could prove highly useful in reducing reliance on China. This agreement, involving 11 countries (Australia, Brunei, Canada, Chile, Japan, Malaysia, Mexico, New Zealand, Peru, Singapore and Vietnam) was rebooted after President Trump removed the United States from the agreement, formerly known as the Trans-Pacific Partnership (TPP), after he came to office.

This agreement will not just increase trade flows but will help integrate supply chains on a regional basis. The Japanese government recently created a $2 billion fund for businesses to examine their supply chains with the intention of lessening their dependence on China. China currently accounts for nearly a quarter of all Japanese imports and in sectors such as automotive parts, it is even more crucial, accounting for nearly 40 percent of imports. The CPTPP may be a path to helping Japanese manufacturers (and others) find alternative sourcing locations (Ralls, 2020).

Further possibilities for supply chain diversification could arise if the other countries that have expressed an interested in joining the CPTPP enter the agreement. Notably South Korea, Thailand, Indonesia, the Philippines and the UK have all been linked with membership.

Interestingly too, the US and China appear open to entering into pacts with their Pacific partners. US Secretary of State Mike Pompeo recently stated the US was looking at how to restructure supply chains with the help of nations such as Japan, Australia, New Zealand and Vietnam. There have also been suggestions that the US might seek to join the CPTPP. China on the other hand has signed up to the Regional Comprehensive Economic Partnership (RCEP) which came into force at the beginning of January 2022. This is a free trade agreement that covers 15 Pacific nations (all 10 of the ASEAN bloc plus Australia, China, Japan, New Zealand and South Korea) and will create the world's largest global free trade agreement. India, an original party to negotiations, has withdrawn.

TOP FIVE POTENTIAL ASIAN 'CHINA PLUS' ALTERNATIVES

India

India has made significant progress in the last decade to modernize its logistics and supply chain industry and, by doing so, deliver strong economic growth. This has included the introduction of a Goods & Services Tax (GST) as well as an electronic waybill for transportation providers crossing state borders which has reduced corruption and transit times. At the same time, the government has looked at ways of making logistics more efficient by addressing bottlenecks, introducing technology and streamlining major transport infrastructure projects, often plagued by delays and mismanagement.

In 2022, the government introduced a National Logistics Policy which has been developed to build on this progress to date. This will include the creation of a unified digital platform that will provide end-to-end visibility for importers and exporters as well as the creation of a multimodal network that will leverage an under-utilized rail system.

However, there is much to do if India is to attract more manufacturing from China – although the country has made a good start (see the case study below on Apple's decision to move some production to India). In terms of logistics, for example, the average turnaround time at an Indian port is 20–40 hours higher than the global average and considerable investment is required in India's port, airport, road and rail infrastructure. Whilst most developed countries have a single-digit logistics cost to GDP ratio, the Indian costs have been in the 14 to 18 percent range for years (Ramachandran, 2022).

APPLE'S INDIA PLAN HELPS DE-RISK SUPPLY CHAIN

In 2022, it was announced that consumer technology company Apple was to manufacture the iPhone 14 in India, marking a significant evolution in its production strategy with implications for its – and its competitors' – supply chains.

Apple's contract manufacturer, Foxconn, already had a plant based in Chennai, but it was typically making older iPhone models with a six-month time lag over global product releases. It is believed that this gap will now narrow to six weeks with a short-term goal of simultaneous release of the iPhone 15 in both markets (Kharpal, 2022).

The move comes as the global tech giant seeks to diversify its production base from China, a market which has seen considerable disruption over the previous years due to zero-Covid lockdown policies. Tensions between the US and China – exacerbated by the controversy of Nancy Pelosi's visit to Taiwan – have also cast doubts over the longer-term prospects of US high-tech companies manu-facturing products in China. For instance, new US legisla-tion has allowed for the banning of the export of advanced semiconductor chip technology to China, although at pre-sent this has not impacted the bulk of the market.

It is believed that in addition to assembly operations, Apple will use more Indian suppliers (presently many intermediate components are sourced from China) helping to develop a production ecosystem and reduce input costs. This will, in turn, encourage other high-tech manufacturers to the country as levels of know-how, a skilled workforce, technology and transport infrastructure improve. Many competitors, such as Samsung, may also follow, keen not to lose competitive advantage in a fast-growing market.

Apple's move shows a high degree of confidence in India both as a design and production hub as well as a consumer market. It also forms part of an industry-wide trend of increasing resilience through 'optionalization' or 'China plus' supply chain strategies. It is not clear what proportion, if any, of Apple's iPhones will be exported to the global market. However, it certainly gives the company more options should manufacturing in China become more difficult or, indeed, impossible.

See also Chapter 2 for more information on the 'Make in India' programme and the government's trade and supply chain policies.

Indonesia

Indonesia is presently in the process of an industry-wide trans-formation aimed at encouraging growth and foreign invest-ment. Its government has adopted a 'Making Indonesia 4.0' programme focusing innovation and development on five key sectors: electronics, chemicals, automotive, food and beverage and textiles. However, whilst the intention may be very sound, considerable progress will need to be made before companies in the market will have Industry 4.0 capabilities. One way to facilitate this would be to remove many of the regulations relating to foreign investment. The easier entry of international companies into Indonesia would allow local businesses to benefit from the transfer of advanced technologies, especially those in the logistics sector which would gain from the intro-duction of digital platforms, GPS and IoT sensor technology, robotics and automation to name just a few.

Whilst offering impressive opportunities, Indonesia has many supply chain and logistics challenges, a fact illustrated by its high proportion of logistics costs to GDP. Despite its strong position in the top ten of the Agility Emerging Market Logistics Index rankings, many in the country believe that progress is not being made as quickly as might be expected, especially given the government's aim to reduce the logistics cost ratio to 17 percent from 26 percent by 2024 (Antara, 2022).

Indonesia has recently adopted a digital National Logistics Ecosystem (NLE) plan which is designed to improve the flow of logistics data and goods, domestically and internationally. Its aim is to simplify business and government processes; enhance public and private collaboration as well as creating a digital pay-ment service. Two of its major goals are to reduce transit times from arrival at port to arrival at warehouse and reduce conges-tion on Indonesia's roads through better planning. However, according to reports, take-up has been slow and connectivity with other platforms low, showing the progress that still has to be made if the government is to fulfill its ambitions.

Indonesia has very close links with China which is its largest trading partner (both in terms of imports and exports) and sec-ond largest provider of foreign direct investment. China's zero tolerance approach to Covid-19 and the disruption this caused for its manufacturing and supply chain industry has had a sig-nificant impact on Indonesia's economy. Whilst 'China plus' sourcing strategies may have mitigated the effects of the policy to some extent, the renewed growth of the Chinese economy; the relaxation on mobility restrictions for Chinese business travelers; increased investment activity and the cessation of 'stop–start' production would far outweigh these benefits.

Malaysia

Malaysia has not been immune to the fallout from the global pandemic and many manufacturers were impacted by the 'whiplash' effect of supply and demand sourcing decisions by their overseas customers. This has resulted in a policy decision by the Malaysian government to place resilience at the heart of its next five-year supply chain plan. This involves a focus on what it calls 'local sourcing facilitation', that is, encouraging and facilitating major manufacturers in the country to use domestic suppliers, often SMEs, rather than those located in other countries. The government believes that a 'buy local' policy will reduce supply chain disruptions such as export bans, border closures or, indeed, the impact of China's zero tolerance approach to Covid-19 which has been so damaging to global value chains across Asia. This will not only increase resilience, but the government believes it will also create 'spillover' benefits cascading down to local businesses in the country.

At the same time as this, investment in transport and digital infrastructure is ongoing from a wide range of sources including government, non-governmental and commercial financial institutions and foreign businesses. The Port of Tanjung Pelepas (PTP) provides a good example of this and in 2022 it announced that it was expanding its capacity by 1 million twenty-foot equivalent units (TEUs) through a joint investment by its owners, Malaysia's MMC group and the Netherlands' APM Terminals (Labrut, 2022).

A significant proportion of Malaysia's foreign investment has also come from China's Belt and Road Initiative (BRI). This has attracted considerable controversy with fears that

Malaysia would fall into a 'debt trap' leaving it beholden to China. Indeed, these fears resulted in a change of government. Nevertheless, since the programme's creation, national and local governments in Malaysia have looked to the BRI for investment in critical infrastructure including ports, rail lines and industrial parks.

As is the case with many emerging markets, Malaysia has developed an 'Industry 4.0' policy to focus its future supply chain strategy. This involves using digital technologies to increase productivity ('by 30 per cent by 2030') whilst improving what it calls its ecological integrity and the quality of life of its people (Shah, 2021). This will involve:

- equipping the workforce with Industry 4.0 skill sets
- developing enhanced digitalized logistics systems to promote interoperability
- increasing the robustness of the regulatory framework to support adoption of transportation and logistics-related technologies
- improving mobility through development and adoption of centralized and open transport-related database, including traffic management
- support R&D for Industry 4.0 technologies to develop low-carbon mobility solutions
- enhance efficiency in cyber security management to mitigate cyber risks

Thailand

Categorized as a Southeast Asian Lost Cost Country (LCC), Thailand's economy has over the past two decades become increasingly integrated within global value chains. Although this has created many opportunities, the trend has meant that its economy has also become highly vulnerable to rising costs and supply chain disruption, such as that resulting from the Covid-19 pandemic. It was particularly affected by the capacity challenges faced by the shipping industry on the transpacific lanes and the resultant high rates.

However, the country has also become a beneficiary of 'China plus' sourcing strategies. Its high-value production eco-systems, especially important in the electronic manufacturing services (EMS), medical equipment and agritech sectors, have provided a ready alternative for companies wishing to migrate away from or complement their Chinese suppliers. Whilst other Southeast Asian countries, such as Vietnam, may have lower labour costs, Thailand is more technologically advanced, especially in the 'green economy' including the manufacture of electric vehicles (EVs). This has provided the country with a significant competitive advantage in the region.

For Thailand to continue its development as a major supply chain hub in the region the government recognizes that it will need to promote further investment in its transport and digital infrastructure at the same time as ensuring inclusive and sus-tainable growth. The government also believes that small and medium-sized enterprises (SMEs) can play a major role in the growth of the economy if it is able to integrate them within GVCs.

The government has developed what it calls 'Thailand 4.0' strategy which has the goal of creating a high-income status country by 2036. This includes prioritizing 12 sectors, not least those of logistics and digital, as well as focusing investment on infrastructure in the Eastern Economic Corridor (EEC) area which it intends will become a gateway to both Southeast Asia and the Asia-Pacific region.

Internationally, Thailand's membership of the ASEAN group of countries and its signing of the Regional Comprehensive Economic Partnership (RCEP) Agreement (which includes ASEAN members, Australia, China, Japan, Republic of Korea and New Zealand) will liberalize market access. As a result, Thai exporters will see lower or zero rate tariffs on tens of thousands of products and they will also benefit from more advantageous rules of origin regulations which will encourage global manufacturers to source within the region.

Vietnam

Vietnam has been very successful in developing its supply chain sector and has been a key beneficiary of 'China plus' strategies. The market has been able to attract many of the world's most prestigious companies to its market, particularly those in the high-tech sector. Electronics and consumer electricals accounted for 42 percent of exports in 2020, soaring from just 13 percent in 2010 (Hoang, 2022).

Apple has been at the forefront of moving production to the market. In 2020 it began planning to expand assembly operations in Vietnam, asking Foxconn to develop its assembly operations in the country. Sony, Samsung and LG have also increased production in Vietnam, building airfreight infrastructure in Hanoi to support their assembly of mobile phones.

Certainly, Vietnam is at the front of the queue for the relocation of electronics production from China. However, whilst the country is exploiting these opportunities, it faces a major challenge to move up the value chain. For example, Apple has created a production ecosystem in the market, sourcing from 21 different companies, but none of these is Vietnamese (Hoang, 2022). Whilst China and India have focused their industrial policy on the creation of national champions, building brands instead of providing services to global OEMs, the Vietnamese market can be characterized as a low-cost assembly location. This may suit global manufacturers, looking for cheap labour in the region as wages and risk rise in China, but it means that it is not able to create value which would enable its manufacturing industry to develop. This will mean that it risks becoming mired in a cycle of decline, faced with:

- high energy usage
- low labour productivity
- low efficiency
- high levels of pollution
- low investment.

There is also the risk that the market could get stuck in the 'middle income gap', where rising labour costs force foreign manufacturers to look elsewhere. If Vietnam is to move further up the rankings it will have to provide investors with a complete package of production ecosystems comprising multiple suppliers, strong ICT links, well-trained workers and good logistics. The latter will be critical to its success with logistics costs presently running at 20 percent of GDP, 7 percentage points higher than the average in Asia (Sarex, 2020). Transport infrastructure projects are often slow to come to fruition plagued by delays, bureaucracy, mismanagement and a culture which penalizes risk taking.

Even though Vietnam is exceptionally well placed to benefit from China's difficulties, the government has much work to do if it is to create a robust industrial environment which will attract high-quality manufacturers and create value adding local suppliers.

CONCLUSION

Whilst China remains the dominant manufacturing force in Asia – and will do for many years to come – there are many opportunities for smaller markets in the region to benefit from changes in Western offshoring strategies. These strategies are being driven both by a better understanding of 'invisible' costs of risk (such as high-impact, low-probability disruptive events) as well as US government policy. As has been discussed in Chapters 4–6, this particularly affects high-tech sectors. However, there are also other factors involved. Rising labour costs are making China's manufacturing sector less competitive and combined with political issues relating to Covid-19, have pushed global companies into looking for lower-cost alternatives.

REFERENCES

Antara (2022) Government targets logistics costs to reach 17 percent of GDP, Antara. Available from https://en.antaranews.com/news /216989/government-targets-logistics- costs-to-reach-17-percent -of-gdp

Hoang, L (2022) Vietnam's battle to climb the global value chain, Nikkei Asia. Available from https://asia.nikkei.com/Spotlight/The -Big-Story/Vietnam-s-battle-to-climb-the- global-value-chain

Hollinger, P, Edgecliffe-Johnson, A, Riordan, P and Li, G (2022) Shanghai lockdown exposes global supply chain strains, Financial Times. Available from www.ft.com/content/9318db50-e0c3-4a27 -9230-55ff59bcc46e

Husband, L (2022) Financial loss, disruption for apparel under China zero-Covid policy, Just-Style.com. Available from www.just-style .com/news/financial-loss-disruption-for- apparel-under-china -zero-covid-policy/

Kharpal, A (2022) Apple begins making the iPhone 14 in India, marking a big shift in its manufacturing strategy, CNBC. Available from www.cnbc.com/2022/09/26/apple- starts-manufacturing-the -iphone-14-in-india.html

Kuo, L and Li, L (2022) Workers flee world's biggest iPhone plant in China over virus restrictions, The Washington Post. Available from www.washingtonpost.com/world/ 2022/11/02/china-foxconn -iphone-factory-zhengzhou-covid/

Labrut, M (2022) Port of Tanjung Pelepas to invest $168m after record 2021, Seatrade Maritime. Available from www.seatrade -maritime.com/ports-logistics/port-tanjung- pelepas-invest-168m -after-record-2021

LaRocco, L (2022) US manufacturing orders from China down 40% in unrelenting demand collapse, CNBC. Available from www .cnbc.com/2022/12/04/manufacturing- orders-from-china-down -40percent-in-demand-collapse.html

LaRocco, L (2022a) China, 'factory of the world', is losing more of its manufacturing and export dominance, latest data shows, CNBC. Available from www.cnbc.com/2022/10/ 20/china-factory-of-the -world-is-losing-its-manufacturing-dominance.html

Ralls, A (2020) CPTPP shows trade pacts have a key role in post-COVID world, Logistics Briefing. Available from www.ti-insight .com/briefs/cptpp-shows-trade-pacts-have-a- key-role-in-post -covid-world/

Ramachandran, R (2022) India's National Logistics Policy: what next? Global Trade. Available from https://www.globaltrademag .com/indias-national-logistics-policy- what-next/

Sarex (2020) Costs for logistics in Vietnam accounted for 20% of GDP, Sarex. Available from https://sarex.com.vn/en/costs-for -logistics-in-vietnam-accounted-for-20-of-gdp/

Shah, S (2021) IR4.0 policy to increase productivity by 30%, The Malaysian Reserve. Available from https://themalaysianreserve .com/2021/07/02/ir4-0-policy-to-increase- productivity-by-30/Ti Insight (2023) Agility Emerging Market Logistics Index 2023, Ti Insight. Available from https://www.agility.com/wp-content /uploads/2023/02/Agility-Emerging-Markets-Logistics-Index -2023-EN.pdf

10

The Reshoring/Near-Sourcing Conundrum

INTRODUCTION

There are many good reasons why manufacturers should consider alternatives to sourcing goods on a global basis. These include risk mitigation (such as avoiding the West Coast port congestion in 2021/22 on transpacific shipping lanes); the desire for more flexibility through the use of JIT transportation; ease of quality control and oversight of regulatory compliance (environmental or worker). The Covid-19 crisis exposed one of the major problems involved in offshored production, namely that if a foreign government wants to ban the export of goods (be they PPE, vaccines or medicines) there is nothing that can be done to prevent it. This has caused many governments to review which sectors are critical to the economic and societal functioning of their country and develop supply chain disruption contingency plans accordingly.

Reshoring of production is not only a key part of engineering resilience, a priority from both a governmental and business point of view, but it has the additional political benefit of creating jobs. It therefore forms an important part of many countries' industrial strategies. Near-sourcing, meanwhile, provides retailers and manufacturers with a supply chain compromise. Labour costs are not as cheap as Asia, but cheaper than Europe/North America and transport times are quicker – essential for some sectors such as 'fast fashion'. This chapter examines how feasible both options are and reviews some of the key near-sourcing markets.

OFFSHORING OR RESHORING: WHICH OPTION?

The decision whether to retain production onshore, move it off-shore or even subsequently reshore has to take into account multiple factors, some related to costs (e.g., wage levels or energy prices), others to do with risk. Some factors are data driven whilst others are more qualitative in nature (e.g., skills and training of the supplier's workforce). In addition to this, the decision is made in a dynamic market environment and these factors are likely to change, sometimes (as in the case of geo-political risk or energy prices) quite quickly.

One research paper identifies that the development of an appropriate supply chain strategy is based on factors categorized by:

- internal business strategy and capabilities
- the business environment in the home market of an enterprise which either 'pushes away' or 'pulls back' production
- the business environment in the destination which either 'pushes away' or 'pulls in' production (Gornostaeva and Barnes, 2015).

As the authors of the research conclude,

> All three sets of factors vary for companies of different size and with different market share, country of origin, business model, type of ownership, capital/labour ratio, and, indeed, industry and activity/product of specialisation are differentiating factors when one tries to understand the logic of companies' behaviour. However, in practice firms' decision making is more complex and often unpredictable so that two companies of very similar profile can take opposite decisions.

In addition to the exogenous costs to take into account, there is also the more qualitative factor of 'management valuation'.

The latter could be based upon the assessment of hidden costs of using a remote, outsourced supplier such as poor quality or communication difficulties, perhaps even loss of intellectual property. Anecdotally, offshoring decisions are often made on the basis of quantifiable costs whilst reshoring can occur as a result of management 'real-world' experience (Gray et al, 2013).

There are many significant practical challenges which must be assessed before deciding whether to retain, reshore or off-shore production. The factors have been categorized in Table 10.1 into those which are harder to measure and which occur at a business level; those operational, financial and logistics factors which can be quantified; and structural economic, governmental or industry factors.

Table 10.1 Onshoring versus offshoring versus reshoring: factors in the decision-making process.

Qualitative/hard to measure supplier business-level factors	Measurable short-term operational, financial and logistics factors	Structural economic, government or industry factors
Ease of communication	Labour costs	Production capacity
Cultural fit	Currency volatility	Manufacturing know-how
Loss of IP/corruption	Tariffs and quotas	Technologies/ automation
Production flexibility	Shipped on time/in full rates	Production ecosystems
Environmental risks and costs	International transport costs and transit time	Government support/ tax breaks
Ethical risks and costs	Border clearance costs and time	Logistics industry maturity
Levels of innovation		Trade finance availability
Product quality		
Proximity to customers		
Customer service		

It should also be noted from the table that there are plenty of actions which management can undertake which would change the balance of the decision. For example, it may be that more effort, experience and expertise in many of the areas listed under the 'Qualitative/hard to measure supplier business-level factors' heading, could result in a better relationship with a remote supplier, for example by addressing internal management inadequacies. Likewise, if management invests effort into quantifying some of these factors, such as risk (which many companies find difficult to assess in financial terms), they will be able to make a better decision.

The fact that many offshoring decisions can be finely balanced has encouraged governments to intervene in the market, for example by imposing tariffs or quotas or providing subsidies. However, often politicians do not understand the dynamics of the market and such moves can have unintended negative consequences.

THE POTENTIAL FOR RESHORING

Evidence to support an industry-wide reshoring trend is notoriously hard to find and, in any case, often controversial due to the way it has become politicized. However, economists at Barclays Bank have estimated that in 2021 companies reshored the equivalent of 350,000 jobs to the USA, compared with just 6,000 jobs in 2010. Moreover, the word 're-shoring' was used 12 times more often in investor conference calls in 2022 than in the same period a year earlier (Hofmann, 2022). This certainly suggests that the trend is real.

If this is indeed the case, the benefits for the US economy will be huge. As previously mentioned, a study undertaken by the US Department of Commerce suggests that US manufacturers import around 20 percent of their intermediate goods compared with 15 percent in 1997. If offshoring were rolled back to the levels last seen in 1997 it would mean that the US would import around $180 billion less product.

In Europe, a survey of media announcements conducted by Eurofound identified that UK companies were most active in reshoring production (Storrie, 2019). It is noticeable that Germany and Spain are much lower down the list than the other big European economies whilst Denmark is high up relative to the size of its GDP (Figure 10.1).

Of these instances of reshoring, apparel manufacturers were the most likely to have reshored their production – most likely to meet retailers' fast fashion requirements (Figure 10.2).

Apart from 'global reorganisation', the survey found that the key reshoring motivations included 'delivery time'; 'automation'; 'poor quality of offshored production' and 'proximity to customers'. These represent some of the 'push' and 'pull' forces already highlighted in Table 10.1. Another factor highlighted by manufacturers was the so-called 'Made in' effect. This refers to the preference for consumers to purchase goods made in a certain country. In the fashion sector, for instance, this is particularly the case for Italian brands. The reputation

Figure 10.1 Number of reshoring cases by country, 2014–2018.

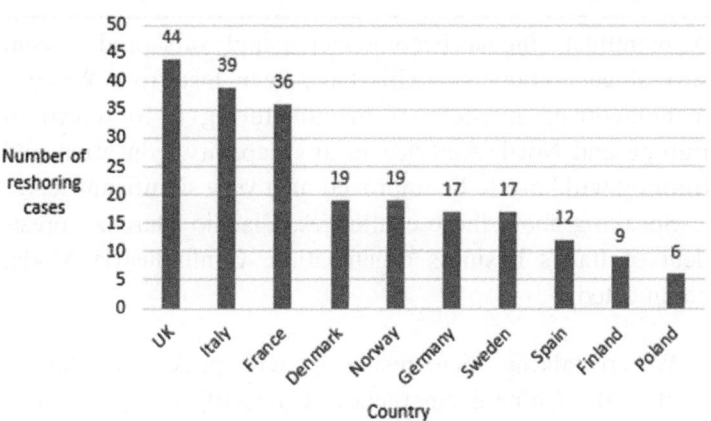

Source: Eurofound: The future of manufacturing in Europe – European Reshoring Monitor 2019.

Figure 10.2 Reshoring case frequency by industry (manufacturing) 2014–2018.

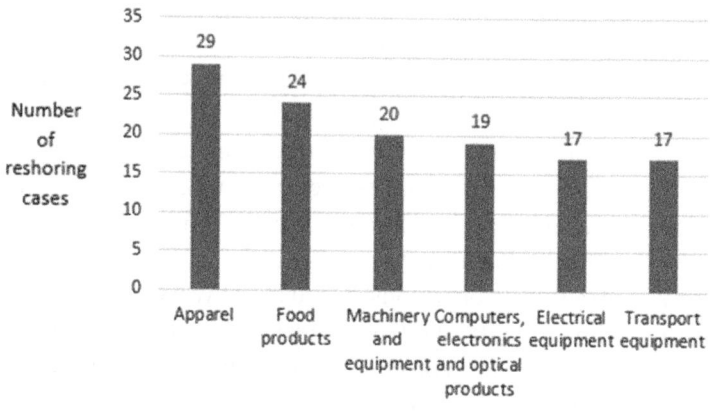

Source: Eurofound: The future of manufacturing in Europe – European Reshoring Monitor, 2019.

for style and quality of clothing produced in Italy is a strong reason to retain or reshore manufacturing to this market.

THE SKILL CHALLENGE

As manufacturing has become increasingly offshored to Asia, several generations of skills have been lost from Western manufacturing markets. If manufacturing is to return to Europe and North America in any capacity, education and training will have to be improved on a very significant scale.

Speaking about these challenges, Claudio Marenzi, president of Italy's business organization, Confindustria Moda, commented,

We are talking about reshoring, with peaks especially after the Chinese emergency [Covid-19], not only for a factor linked to the availability of production sourcing, but also to improve lead time, i.e. delivery times.

However, the reflection must keep in mind that some production steps in Italy no longer exist because they are decentralized over the years and therefore we would not even have the skills in the short term.

(Mina, 2020)

One of the key problems in attracting talent to the industry is that parts of manufacturing (such as clothing and textiles) have a poor public perception due to workers' low wages and harsh conditions. This has caused scandals such as that reported in the global media related to suppliers of UK brand Boohoo, reinforcing the 'low pay, low skill' perception (Butler, 2021).

THE NEAR-SOURCING ALTERNATIVE

As previously discussed, many manufacturers are looking to locate their suppliers in near-sourcing markets as a compromise between optimizing 'speed to market' and using low-cost, remote suppliers based in Asia. This trend has benefited manufacturing locations at the peripheries of major consumer markets providing shorter transit times, easier management control in terms of quality, sustainability and ethics, whilst at the same time having lower costs than those in developed markets. For European manufacturers and retailers these include North Africa (e.g. Morocco and Egypt) and for those based in North America, Mexico and Central America.

Looking at landed costs (i.e., taking into account cost of transport), it can be cheaper to use a near-sourcing supplier than one which is Asia-based. This is even before other benefits are taken into account such as the ability to gain 'full-price sell through'. This latter point is very important in sectors such as fast fashion where the ability to provide 'fresh' product to consumers and thereby achieve non-discounted (or at least only marginally discounted) prices is critical. In other words, maintaining the economic value of a product.

Selected European near-sourcing locations

Morocco and Tunisia

Both these countries have become important near-sourcing markets, helped by the development of the Euromed partnership across the region, formed in 2008. In addition to providing a free trade area (for goods with the requisite Rules of Origin), this partnership has also facilitated the integration of European and North African transport networks (as well as those of other countries in the region).

Customs arrangements allow for shipments to be inspected and sealed at or close to the factory of origin before transport direct to the European customer. The transit time can be as short as 3–4 days to Northern Europe, using regular and frequent ferries, less if the customer is in Spain (Spanish-based Inditex, one of the world's largest clothing groups, has a considerable number of Moroccan suppliers).

Suppliers in these countries have been serving the European market for many decades and have therefore built up well-established processes, technologies, networks as well as links with customs organizations. They have been integrated into West European supply chains, and this has been helped by the ease with which purchasing managers can travel to see their suppliers and oversee quality control.

Egypt

Egypt has been one of Africa's success stories over the past decade, outperforming most markets in the Middle East, North Africa and sub-Saharan region, despite the impact which Covid-19 has had upon its economy, especially tourism. The country now accounts for over a fifth of the continent's manufacturing value add and the government's business-friendly approach has been particularly successful at attracting international investors, not least in the high-tech sector. Despite being one of Africa's largest markets, its focus lies very much on trade with Europe. Links with the rest of the continent, with the exception of its North African neighbours, are weak and only 15 percent of its exports overall are shipped to African destinations (*Egypt Today*, 2022).

The development of industrial parks, both public and private, will play an important role in the country's economic growth. Many of these parks form part of specialized sector clusters, such as furniture or technology, helping to develop an ecosystem of relevant competences and foster co-ordination between companies. The government hopes that they will facilitate the development of continental value chains.

The Egyptian government has embraced moves to digitize and liberalize its trade processes. Driven by the Ministry of Finance, a new system has been implemented designed to cut clearance times, including a risk management functionality which will allow for the earlier release of goods through a 'green channel' for authorized economic operators.

Turkey

Turkey enjoys close trading relations with the EU, underpinned by access to its internal market through a customs union. The country's large, experienced labour pool and low costs, combined with its proximity to large consumer markets, means that suppliers can be closely integrated into European supply chains. Higher production costs in Turkey compared with Asia are balanced by the benefits of shorter transit times and the ability to react faster to market developments.

There are other specific advantages to using suppliers in Turkey, including its resources of raw materials which it also exports to North Africa, East Africa and Central Europe. It is integrated into other near-sourcing markets throughout the region, supplying manufacturers, for example, in Morocco or Bulgaria. The set of skills, technologies, access to raw materials and upstream and downstream capabilities is likely to increase Turkey's position as Europe's most important near-sourcing location unless, as mentioned earlier, political factors interfere.

NEAR-SOURCING: MEXICO'S
BIG OPPORTUNITY?

For decades, large parts of the Mexican economy have been integrated within US supply chains leading to economic growth particularly in border cities and states. The Covid-19 pandemic has encouraged a new wave of investment in cross-border factories as manufacturers have sought to avoid the problems on trans-Pacific routes caused by congestion, delays and exceptionally high freight rates. With around 82 percent of exports to the US routed by road and rail (BTS, 2023), land-based logistics networks were not as badly affected as those reliant on movements of containers through the West Coast ports, although Mexican shippers were certainly not immune from the wider supply chain chaos caused by bottlenecks and congestion across the region.

Setting aside the short-term disruption which had largely subsided by the end of 2022, it would seem evident that the Mexican economy will significantly benefit from the deteriorating relationship between the US and China. However, this will only occur if the Mexican government is able to build a more attractive business case for foreign investment. Despite being the fifteenth largest recipient of FDI in 2019 (World Bank, 2023), its record in this respect is mixed, as indicated by the stagnating of exports to the USA even prior to the Covid-19 pandemic.

Advantageous location

Mexico's proximity and access to the US market through the United States-Mexico-Canada Agreement (USMCA) (the successor to the North America Free Trade Agreement (NAFTA)) has long made it a near-sourcing location for manufacturers looking to supply the US market cheaply, quickly and with easier oversight of production processes and quality control than offshoring. Moving goods from Mexico to the USA takes only days compared with several weeks spent in transit from

China. Tariff increases on goods imported to the USA from China have reinforced Mexico's position as an attractive alternative: the composite tariff rate imposed on Mexican goods is just 0.04 percent compared with 19.2 percent on Chinese imports (Alix, 2022).

However, the market is far from straight forward and Mexico has challenges to overcome if it is to maximize the opportunities which 'China plus' sourcing strategies offer.

Labour

The low cost of labour in Mexico is one of the main reasons why foreign manufacturers have chosen to base their production operations in the country. According to Statista, the average manufacturing industry wage in 2020 in Mexico was $4.82 per hour, comparing with $6.50 in China (Statista, 2023). The comparable wage in the USA is closer to $23 per hour (Trading Economics, 2023). Mexico also has an abundant and growing resource of labour with an estimated 7 million people available for work. However, wages are rising both as a result of market forces and government policy. The statutory minimum wage jumped by 20 percent in 2022 and pension reforms will increase employer contributions (Crowley, 2022).

The government will have an important role to play in creating a well-educated and skilled workforce. This will help employers as well as workers who will benefit from longer-term and better remunerated positions within the formal jobs market. Growth is presently being constrained by a lack of managerial calibre candidates with manufacturers competing to hire from a small top-talent pool. The market also lacks skills which would allow the economy to break into high-tech, advanced manufacturing such as semiconductors.

This lack of skills at the upper end of the market, coupled with an economy competing on the basis of low cost, low value adding production capabilities means Mexico risks falling into the 'middle income trap' as rising wages force manufacturers to look elsewhere in the Latin America region for cheaper near-sourcing opportunities. To prevent this the government will need to look at making the employment market more flexible at the same time as creating a high value adding manufacturing environment, leveraging other advantages such as its proximity to the US market whilst investing heavily in value-adding capabilities and training.

There are also issues related to labour laws. Whilst the government has a reputation for enforcing regulations related to the treatment of workers employed by foreign businesses, there is the view that it is less effective when it comes to the 'informal' sector, which accounts for more than half of the labour force. This has created a level of instability in the employment market which in turn is fostering adversarial relations between unions and businesses.

Security and corruption

The security situation in Mexico is one of the greatest headwinds to economic growth. One of the biggest risks related to the supply chain involves the theft of cargo from trucks *en route* to the border with the US. Drug cartels also target legitimate shipments in which to infiltrate illicit goods.

Corruption is a major problem. Government officials, including customs officers and law enforcement agents, can work in collaboration with organized crime. Mexico's position in Transparency International's Corruption Perception Index has fallen every year since 2012 and it is now ranked 124 out of 180 countries.

Critical resources

With the US increasingly keen to find alternative sources of critical minerals to lessen its dependence on China, Mexico has an opportunity to increase its supply of several important raw materials essential in the 'green economy'. These include fluorspar, strontium, gold, manganese and lithium. However, the present government, led by President Andrés Manuel López Obrador, is in the process of nationalizing parts of the mining industry, specifically that related to the extraction of lithium, which would limit foreign investment in the future. Despite this, there may be other opportunities for foreign participation such as the development of upstream refining operations, integrating within US battery electric vehicle (BEV) supply chains.

Government investment policy

The Mexican government is prioritizing investment in transport infrastructure, with a financial package of $38.6 billion planned in 2022 to improve roads, bridges and railways. In addition, the US government has committed to invest $1.4 billion to build and modernize land ports on the US–Mexican border, matching that promised by President Obrador (Bnamericas, 2022).

However, the criticism has been levelled that Mexico has the lowest level of public investment amongst OECD countries. The government also intends to spread its investment across the country, not just on the regions which already have a focus on manufacturing and logistics, but poorer areas especially to the south. Although politically popular, this has meant a misalignment between industry needs and the infrastructure development which may not be in the long-term economic interests of the country given its limited resources.

A trusted partner

Despite the tensions created by the problem of illegal immigration and security concerns, relations between Mexico and USA remain strong with close economic, social and cultural ties.

CONCLUSION

When politicians in the West talk about the potential for the development of reshoring and near-sourcing models, they often point to the success of fashion retailer Inditex, not least for its agility and flexibility in dealing with the Covid-19 crisis. Inditex may come to be seen as an example of what retailers can achieve using local supply chain structures rather than depending on global suppliers. As well as its strong online presence, Inditex relied on local manufacturing in countries such as Portugal, Spain and Morocco; a dense European network based around centres in Spain to re-distribute items to outlets worldwide; and stores which doubled up as e-commerce fulfilment centres.

However, reshoring and near-sourcing will only ever be components of a more complicated supply chain mix. The cost and capability advantages which suppliers in China and the rest of Asia have over rivals in closer proximity to the main markets in Europe and North America is likely to mean that reshoring/near-sourcing remains only a limited part of the market for many years to come.

In fact, the perception of the global market as a dichotomy of West (developed) and East (developing) markets already looks out of date. The reality is much more complex as some of the world's largest consumer markets are now located in Asia. The strategy required to supply Europe and North America will need to remain dynamic; taking into account shifts in currencies, labour costs, transport costs, ethical and environmental risks and trade policy. Global manufacturers have to achieve this whilst at the same time increasing their presence in faster growing emerging markets. This may well be the more important challenge of the next decade.

REFERENCES

Alix Partners (2022) Revisiting Mexico: A critical link in the supply chain, Alix Partners. Available from https://docs.alixpartners.com/view/459379855/

Bnamericas (2022) Mexico to invest US$38.6bn in road, rail infrastructure in 2022, Bnamericas. Available from https://www.bnamericas.com/en/news/mexico-to-invest-   us386bn-in-road-rail-infrastructure-in-2022

BTS (2023) North American Transborder Freight up 13.9% in October 2022 from October 2021, Bureau of Transportation Statistics. Available from www.bts.gov/newsroom/north-american-transborder-freight-139-october-2022-october-2021

Butler, S (2021) Boohoo accused of failing to improve working conditions in its supply chain, The Guardian. Available from www.theguardian.com/business/2021/jun/18/boohoo-accused-of-failing-to-improve-working-conditions-in-its-supply-chain

Crowley, E (2022) Mexico's nearshoring potential: weighing opportunities and risks, Supply Chain Quarterly. Available from www.supplychainquarterly.com/articles/7256-   mexicos-nearshoring-potential-weighing-opportunities-and-risks

Egypt Today (2022) Trade minister: we seek to increase Egypt's exports to Africa, Egypt Today. Available from www.egypttoday.com/Article/3/120930/Trade-minister-We-   seek-to-increase-Egypt-s-exports-to

Gornostaeva, G. and Barnes, D (2015) Offshoring and Backshoring in the British Fashion and Apparel Industry: A Literature Review, Westminster Research. Available from https://core.ac.uk/download/pdf/161103804.pdf

Gray, J, Skowronski, K, Esenduran, G and Rungtusanatham, J (2013) The reshoring phenomenon: what supply chain academics ought to know and should do, Ohio State University. Available from https://doi.org/10.1111/jscm.12012

Hofmann, J (2022) The reshoring dividend, Investors Chronicle. Available from www. investorschronicle.co.uk/ideas/2022/09/22/the-reshoring-dividend/

Mina, D (2020) It's reshoring time, MF Fashion. Available from https://www.mffashion. com/news/it-s-reshoring-time-202003051950501061

Statista (2023) Manufacturing labor costs per hour for China, Vietnam, Mexico from 2016 to 2020, Statista. Available from

www.statista.com/statistics/744071/manufacturing-labor-costs
-per-hour-china-vietnam-mexico/

Storrie, D (2019) The future of manufacturing in Europe, Publications
Office of the European Union, Luxembourg. Available from
https://www.epma.com/dm-industry- news/833-eurofound-report
-future-of-manufacturing-in-europe-april-2019/file

Trading Economics (2023) United States average hourly wages in
manufacturing, Trading Economics. Available from https://
tradingeconomics.com/united-states/wages-in- manufacturing

World Bank (2023) Foreign direct investment, net inflows – Mexico,
World Bank DataBank. Available from https://data.worldbank.org
/indicator/BX.KLT.DINV.CD. WD?locations=MX

11

The Impact of Green Legislation on Supply Chains

INTRODUCTION

In many people's minds, the development of global supply chains predicated on low-cost labour and cheap transport has led to the unnecessary movement of goods around the world, resulting in unsustainable levels of carbon emissions.

Examples are often used to show how intermediate products within global value chains cross multiple international borders before final assembly or processing and then subsequent shipment thousands of miles to end users in Europe or North America. The carbon emissions involved in such supply chains are often compared unfavourably with a local or regional movement, especially if air cargo is involved.

There are two components to this criticism. The first relates to the carbon footprint of the transport required to connect global production facilities and distribution hubs with customers on a worldwide basis. The second relates to the lower environmental standards often employed in the markets to which production has been offshored. However, as we have discussed elsewhere in the book, environmental concerns have also become intertwined with politically motivated protectionist policies.

THE IMPACT OF ENVIRONMENTAL LEGISLATION ON INTERNATIONAL SHIPPING

Arguably the single biggest factor in the globalization of the world's markets has been the containerization of the shipping industry which occurred from the 1950s onwards. Advances in ship-building technology, the unitization of shipments and a transformation of operating models has enabled the leverage of economies of scale which in turn has depressed freight rates. This has allowed manufacturers in the West to outsource production to low-cost labour markets in Asia.

Whilst Western consumers have enjoyed lower-cost products and Asian markets higher levels of employment, there have been negative consequences, not least in terms of carbon emissions. The International Maritime Organization has estimated that CO_2 emissions from shipping account for 2.89 percent of global emissions (2018), a total of 1056 million tonnes. Unlike in other sectors, these are continuing to rise – the organization estimates that, if nothing is done to curb emissions, they could grow 50–250 percent by 2050 (IMO, 2020).

This has encouraged organizations such as the International Maritime Organization (IMO), which regulates the shipping industry, and governments to take action to 'price in' external costs to the environment. The European Union has taken the lead in this respect by legislating to include international shipping within its Emissions Trading Scheme (ETS). Established in 2005, the ETS is designed to reduce emissions of carbon dioxide, nitrous oxide and perfluorocarbons (PFCs) in some sectors by way of the 'cap and trade' principle.

CAP AND TRADE

The EU ETS works on the 'cap and trade' principle. A cap is set on the total amount of certain greenhouse gases that can be emitted by installations covered by the system. The cap is reduced over time so that total emissions fall.

Within the cap, companies receive or buy emission allowances, which they can trade with one another as needed. They can also buy limited amounts of international credits from emission-saving projects around the world. The limit on the total number of allowances available ensures that they have a value.

After each year a company must surrender enough allowances to cover all its emissions, otherwise heavy fines are imposed. If a company reduces its emissions, it can keep the spare allowances to cover its future needs or else sell them to another company that is short of allowances.

Trading brings flexibility that ensures emissions are cut where it costs least to do so. A robust carbon price also promotes investment in clean, low-carbon technologies (EC, 2021).

In December 2022, it was agreed by the European Parliament that shipping emissions would be included within the ETS scheme, although obligations would be phased in over a number of years, with the regulations being fully enforced for 100 percent of emissions in 2026. All emissions from intra-EU voyages would fall within its scope as well as 50 percent of emissions from extra-EU voyages.

Pricing in externalities will have an immediate impact on shipping freight rates, providing a further headwind to the global flows of goods around the world. This is not necessarily the primary aim of the ETS scheme, which is to reduce carbon emissions through the adoption of green technologies in the sector, but it is certainly likely to be a short-term impact. According to Danish shipping line, Maersk, 'The cost of compliance with the ETS will likely be significant therefore impacting the cost of shipping'. It intends to pass on the costs to customers through a surcharge on each forty foot equivalent (FFE) container. In July 2022, it estimated these costs to amount to €170 for each dry FFE between Far East and North Europe and €255 for each refrigerated container (Maersk, 2022). Given that spot rates on this route in December 2022 were roughly around $2000 per dry FFE, this surcharge amounts to an increase in rates of just under 10 percent.

The extension of the ETS has certainly not been universally welcomed. Guy Platten, secretary general of International Chamber of Shipping, commented:

> Other than as an ideological revenue raising exercise, which will greatly upset the EU's trading partners, it's difficult to see what extending the EU ETS to shipping will achieve towards reducing CO_2, particularly as the proposal only covers about 7.5% of shipping's global emissions. This could seriously put back climate negotiations [at the IMO] for the remaining 92.5% of shipping emissions.

He went on to say, 'It is clear that there will need to be an independent impact assessment of these proposals as soon as possible, to ensure that we are not sleepwalking towards unmanageable costs for global trade' (ICS, 2021).

One of the fears which has been raised is that the ETS may be an additional cost to a proposed carbon tax on shipping fuels, a measure presently being discussed by the IMO. Japan, for example, has suggested that the shipping industry pays $56 per tonne of CO_2 from 2025 to 2030, raising in excess of $50 billion a year. The money raised would be invested in green technologies to help with decarbonization projects. Other suggestions have included charging ships which fall below a certain level of carbon efficiency.

Whilst it is not the intention of this review of environmental legislation to examine its merits, it is important to highlight that it will have implications for shipping policy. At the very least, significant costs will be passed on to the customer (retailer or manufacturer) and then ultimately the customer. Combined with other environmental levies (such as surcharges related to the use of sulphur in fuels) this will mean that intercontinental transport costs re-balance and make the model of remote manufacturing shipments less attractive. This must be viewed in the context of the range of global headwinds examined in Chapter 1 – individually not enough to swing the pendulum back towards reshoring of manufacturing, but, combined with other costs, increasingly significant. As with the Carbon Border Adjustment Mechanism discussed below, the motives behind the EU's efforts to reduce carbon emissions have been called into question. Although this may be cynical, it is reasonable to ask whether the EU would have been quite so keen if there had been significant costs passed on to its members rather than tax benefits.

EU'S CARBON BORDER ADJUSTMENT MECHANISM (CBAM)

The intervention which has attracted the most criticism is the EU's Carbon Border Adjustment Mechanism (CBAM). This new levy on imports (part of its 'Fit for 55' package – the target to reduce carbon emissions by 55 percent relative to 1990 levels) has been developed to address concerns in the EU that manufacturers in the region are being penalised by stringent environmental regulations which companies in the rest of the world do not have to follow. This, according to politicians, has put the EU's manufacturing industry at a disadvantage, encouraged outsourcing and resulted in so-called 'carbon leaking' i.e., carbon-reduction efforts in the EU have been offset by an increase in carbon-intensive production in other parts of the world. Under the proposed rules importers will need to surrender carbon allowances corresponding to the products' carbon footprint (de Jong, 2022).

The CBAM will result in a levy being charged on imports of the most carbon-intensive goods which will, in the view of the EU, create a level-playing field for EU manufacturers and reduce the pressure on companies to offshore production to lower-cost markets. Commencing in October 2023, importers of certain goods (iron and steel, cement, fertilizers, aluminium, electricity and hydrogen) will need to comply with certain reporting obligations. Following this, 'free allowances' will be phased out in conjunction with the implementation of the EU emissions trading system (ETS) although a time scale has not yet been established.

As Jozef Síkela, Minister of Industry and Trade of Czechia, commented,

> The Carbon Border Adjustment Mechanism is a key part of our climate action. This mechanism promotes the import of goods by non-EU businesses into the EU which fulfil the high climate standards applicable in the 27 EU member states. This will ensure a balanced treatment of such imports and is designed to encourage our partners in the world to join the EU's climate efforts.
>
> *(EC, 2022)*

As he makes clear, those companies which adhere to best practice in the rest of the world should not be affected.

This positive interpretation of the new tax is mirrored by the International Monetary Fund (IMF) which has commented, 'An international carbon price floor is analogous to a global minimum corporate tax…Such a floor would discourage emissions and alleviate competitiveness concerns' (Gaspar et al, 2022).

However, as might be expected, the initiative has proved highly controversial amongst the EU's trading partners. It is being seen at the very least as an attempt to impose a set of rules on the rest of the world, using its huge import market as a lever. At the very worst it is viewed as an effort to increase barriers to international trade in order to protect its manufacturing industry already struggling with high energy prices. As discussed in Chapter 7, many carbon intensive, high energy using manufacturers are looking to move production to lower-cost markets and re-import goods back to the EU from these new locations. The issues of high energy costs (driven by geo-political concerns rather than climate change) and carbon reduction targets have become conflated which has, in turn, resulted in mistrust and obloquy.

Is CBAM WTO compliant?

The traditional arbiter of international trade disputes has been the World Trade Organization (WTO). At the heart of the argument is whether European products are being treated more favourably than foreign imports, which would run counter to WTO rules. The EU argues that both domestically produced goods, which face a 'cap and trade' regime under its ETS and imports are being treated similarly. This argument may be flawed as although the WTO recognizes that 'border tax adjustments' are a legitimate method of creating a level-playing field, CBAM is not a tax but a regulatory scheme. The technicalities of the application of WTO rules could result in many years of legal arguments (Benson, 2022).

The EU's scheme may also be incompatible with WTO rules due to the inclusion of export rebates for EU producers in contravention to the Agreement on Subsidies and Countervailing Duties (Reinsch, 2022). This would seem an obvious attempt to make EU exporters more competitive on the global market – a blatant political rather than environmental step – and one which will face considerable opposition.

One way to overcome a fragmented, nationally focused and potentially discriminatory approach to carbon adjustment policies would be to negotiate a new WTO agreement which sets out what members can and cannot do in the context of carbon border taxes. Alternatively, this could fall under the remit of the United Nation's Framework Convention on Climate Change. However, the length of time this would take and past experience of previous ill-fated negotiations would suggest that countries and regions, such as the EU, will pursue their own agendas, leading to considerable tension and the prospect of higher trade barriers.

Impact of CBAM on other developing countries

One of the primary complaints of developing countries is that their industries will be penalized for the costs of climate change, even though they are not responsible for global warming. Many African, Asian and Latin American economies are highly dependent on exports of goods to the EU targeted by the CBAM such as fertilizers, cement and aluminium. As an example, figures developed by the EU itself suggest that the border adjustment charge would increase the cost of Mozambique's aluminium exports per tonne by 39 percent. The Center for Global Development (CGD) estimates that this would mean a fall in Mozambique's GDP by 1.6 percent given the importance of the sector to its economy, although the CGD believes that the impact of CBAM would more likely result in localized job losses in developing countries rather than widespread economic downturn. In particular, the CGD says that, '...a carbon border tax has the potential to inhibit development of the middle-income countries that export these goods' (Pleek et al, 2022). A report in the *Financial Times* quotes one diplomat as saying that the policy could result in the 'deindustrialization' of African nations exporting to the EU (Hancock, 2022).

Discontent was laid bare at the COP27 meeting in 2022 where a statement by the 'BASIC' group of countries – Brazil, South Africa, India and China – was delivered which stated, 'Unilateral measures and discriminatory practices, such as carbon border taxes, that could result in market distortion and aggravate the trust deficit amongst parties, must be avoided'. (Weko, 2022). The 'trust deficit' refers to the perception that the costs of climate change and its responsibility is being transferred to developing countries from the West. One such possible trade 'distortion' includes the diversion or 'dumping' of commodities in markets outside Europe once the mechanism has been implemented. Brazilian manufacturers have highlighted this risk as a possible unintended consequence of the policy as they fear that their domestic market could become awash with cheap Chinese steel formerly destined for Europe.

However, it is China which will be most impacted by CBAM with about 2 percent of imports being affected, equivalent to €6.5bn in 2019 (Deloitte, 2022). The measures would also have an impact on some of the products required to drive the renewable energy industry, such as aluminium, cobalt and steel. Although China has its own ETS, this relates to carbon intensity, not volumes, and nationally only covers electricity generation. Consequently, it is unlikely that the EU will take this into account when assessing the levy to be paid by importers of Chinese products falling within its remit. That being said, the EU is helping the Chinese authorities to develop the ETS further and this has helped to mitigate political fallout from the scheme.

Entrenching bureaucracy

Another criticism of the CBAM is that it will create an innovation-crushing bureaucracy, resulting from the perceived primacy of the EU's regulatory approach to carbon reduction through its ETS scheme. As Maureen Hinman, Cofounder and Executive Chair of Silverado, comments, 'By prejudicing other potentially more efficacious emissions reduction instruments, the CBAM could have an unintended chilling effect on novel carbon reduction efforts in third countries' (Benson, 2022). In other words, the imposition of a new trading regime may mean that other more effective methods of reducing carbon emissions (regulatory and market-based) could be ignored.

There are also concerns over how effectively the regulation of the system can be enforced. Carbon allowance thresholds and certificates will have to be computed, evaluated and the exchange managed. Dispute mechanisms will have to be put in place not only between the EU and importers but on an intra-EU basis, as national thresholds within the ETS will be involved.

The response of the USA

The US first raised concerns about the CBAM in 2020, directly questioning its legality at the WTO. It has been estimated that $1.1 billion of US exports would be affected under the mechanism, a relatively small proportion of the total $231 billion of exports to the EU in 2020 (Jarsulic,

2020). However, this will change as the scope of CBAM expands to include the import of US chemicals which are relatively more carbon emission intensive than European equivalents.

Whilst pursuing redress through the WTO's arbitration process is one option, legislation has also been introduced to create the USA's own version of CBAM as a way of countering its effects. In June 2022, the Clean Competition Act (CCA) was introduced by two Democratic senators (developing an earlier bill, the Fair, Affordable, Innovative, and Resilient Transition and Competition Act), although getting the necessary bipartisan support will depend on the details of the legislation, especially those regarding the implementation of a domestic carbon floor price.

The carbon price is fundamental to the Act as it would allow the mechanism (placing a tax on imports to the USA) to be WTO compliant (in a way which the CBAM is presently not). According to law company, Wiley,

> The amount of the border tax is based on multiplying the carbon emission content of the imported product by the domestic environmental cost in the US sector for that product. In short, the tax approximates the domestic carbon costs that foreign manufacturers would have borne had they produced their goods in the United States.
>
> *(Wiley, 2021)*

If passed, the tax will apply to goods produced by industries including fossil fuels, refined petroleum products, petrochemicals, fertilizer, hydrogen, adipic acid, cement, iron and steel, aluminium, glass, pulp and paper and ethanol. The scheme would be phased in from 2024.

Unlike CBAM, the CCA would exempt least developed countries as well as countries which do not have similar border adjustment schemes but which enforce laws and regulations that are as least as ambitious in terms of carbon reduction as the US.

ENVIRONMENTAL AND
SOCIETAL ENGINEERING

Whilst trade has always been inextricably tied up with politics and economics, it is only relatively recently that environmental and ethical considerations have become important factors in measuring the success or otherwise of globalization.

US Trade Representative, Katherine Tai, has made the enforcement of environmental standards a priority, for example, highlighting two issues: the plight of the vaquita, a cetacean critically endangered by illegal fishing in waters around Mexico and illegal logging in Vietnam. The aim is to use trade regulations to keep illegally harvested or traded goods out of the supply chain.

Beyond this, trade has now become a conduit for the promotion of a range of societal objectives. According to Tai, the Biden administration is designing a trade policy that will, 'consider the intersection of race/ethnicity, gender, age, education, income, disability, orientation, region, and underserved communities' (USTR, 2022).

Although there are very few who would argue against any of the outcomes aspired to by administrators such as Ambassador Tai, it must be understood that trade is now being used as a lever to pressurize partners into falling into line with Western doctrine in much the same way as China has used trade and investment to promote its own interests. Whilst many reading this book will seek to discriminate between the two goals – one being wholly positive whilst the other is brazenly geo-political – the mechanism used is essentially the same.

CONCLUSION

The EU's effort to 'level the playing field' through the implementation of a carbon border adjustment levy has provoked widespread criticism from its trade partners, especially the USA as well as a host of countries in the developing world. However, it has also prompted many countries to engage positively with the concept, developing their own versions of emissions trading systems which would allow exports to be exempted from the EU's mechanism. A key reason for this is that this will mean 'tax' revenues stay at home rather than being transferred into the European Union.

Protectionism of any sort has a negative impact on the global flows of goods and this will be most definitely the case with CBAM, the proposed CCA and other such schemes. Their entire existence is based on discouraging manufacturers from unbundling and outsourcing parts of their production to cheaper locations which don't meet the stringent environmental restrictions being placed upon them. Whilst the original aim for CBAM may well have been to reduce carbon leakage, it is inevitable that in many parts of the world it looks like a convenient political tool to stem the exodus of Europe's heavy industry to regions with cheaper sources of energy. On top of this, many emerging markets regard carbon border adjustment as a levy on the poorest countries even though they are not the ones responsible for global warming. In order to counter these criticisms, it may be politic for the EU to look at using monies raised by the mechanism to help emerging markets implement climate mitigation programmes.

REFERENCES

Benson (2022) CBAM precedents: experts weigh in, Center for Strategic and International Studies. Available from www.csis.org /analysis/cbam-precedents-experts-weigh

De Jong, S (2022) The EU's Carbon Border Adjustment Mechanism, American University, Washington. Available from https://www .american.edu/sis/centers/transatlantic-policy/07252022-the-eus -carbon-border-adjustment-mechanism.cfm

Deloitte (2022) CBAM and its implications for companies in China, Deloitte. Available from www2.deloitte.com/cn/en/pages/risk/ articles/esg-cbam-china-implications.html

EC (2021) Questions and Answers – Emissions Trading – Putting a Price on carbon, European Commission. Available from https://ec .europa.eu/commission/presscorner/detail/en/qanda_21_3542

EC (2022) EU climate action: provisional agreement reached on Carbon Border Adjustment Mechanism (CBAM), European Council. Available from www.consilium.europa.eu/en/press/press -releases/2022/12/13/eu-climate-action-provisional-agreement -reached- on-carbon-border-adjustment-mechanism-cbam

Gaspar, V et al (2022) Tax coordination can lead to a fairer, greener global economy, International Monetary Fund. Available from www.imf.org/en/Blogs/Articles/2022/04/ 12/blog041222-sm2022 -fm-ch2

Hancock, A (2022) EU's trading partners accuse bloc of protectionism over carbon tax plan, Financial Times, London. Available from www.ft.com/content/67c1ea12-7495- 43ff-9718-7189cef48fd6

ICS (2021) EU overreach threatens to sink shipping's decarbonisation efforts, warns ICS, International Chamber of Shipping. Available from www.ics-shipping.org/press- release/eu-overreach-threatens -to-sink-shippings-decarbonisation-efforts/

IMO (2020) Fourth Greenhouse Gas Study 2020, International Maritime Organisation. Available from https://www.imo.org/en /OurWork/Environment/Pages/Fourth-IMO-   Greenhouse-Gas -Study-2020.aspx

Jarsulic, M (2020) What the European Union's proposed trade tax on carbon means for the United States, American Progress. Available from www.americanprogress.org/ article/european -unions-proposed-trade-tax-carbon-means-united-states/" www . americanprogress.org/article/european-unions-proposed-trade -tax-carbon-means- united-states/

Maersk (2022) EU Emissions Trading System (ETS) – latest developments, Maersk. Available from www.maersk.com/news/articles/2022/07/12/eu-ets-latest-developments

Pleek, S, Denton, F and Mitchell, I (2022) An EU tax on African carbon – assessing the impact and ways forward, Center for Global Development. Available from www.cgdev. org/blog/eu-tax -african-carbon-assessing-impact-and-ways-forward

Reinsch, W (2022) Trade tools for climate: transatlantic carbon border adjustments, Center for Strategic and International Studies. Available from www.csis.org/analysis/trade-tools -climate-transatlantic-carbon-border-adjustments

USTR (2022) One Year In, Ambassador Katherine Tai is Advancing President Biden's Trade Agenda and Getting Results for American Workers, Office of the United States Trade Representative. Available from https://ustr.gov/about-us/policy-offices/ press -office/fact-sheets/2022/march/fact-sheet-one-year-ambassador -katherine-tai-   advancing-president-bidens-trade-agenda-and -getting

Weko, S (2022) The future for global trade in a changing climate, Chatham House. Available from www.chathamhouse.org/2022/12 /future-global-trade-changing-climate

Wiley (2021) Democrats introduce carbon border adjustment legislation, Wiley. Available from www.wiley.law/alert -Democrats-Introduce-Carbon-Border-Adjustment- Legislation

12

How Ethics and Politics Will Determine Future Supply Chains

INTRODUCTION

One of the defining features of the next decade in terms of the supply chain management strategies of global retailers and manufacturers will be the pressure that they will come under to justify their sourcing decisions from an ethical perspective. This could have systemic implications for global supply chains not least due to the growing political gulf between China and the West.

RETAINING RESPONSIBILITY

There has been growing pressure on global manufacturers and retailers to demonstrate that they implement ethical policies when it comes to the treatment of their suppliers' workers. No longer is it morally acceptable for manufacturers to outsource production or for retailers to purchase goods from suppliers without having full visibility of these issues.

One of the consequences of the unbundling and outsourcing of manufacturing processes has been the fragmentation and increased complexity of supplier networks. This is especially pronounced when outsourcing to production locations in emerging markets as remoteness and a lack of familiarity with the market can make it difficult for many companies to operate effective oversight.

Even if there is a willingness to increase visibility of working practices and conditions in lower tiers of suppliers, the task is often challenging and made more difficult by an unwillingness of Tier 1 suppliers to cooperate. A study by the Ethical Trade Initiative found that whereas respondents to a survey thought that it was 'Very Likely' that 10 percent of Tier 1 suppliers could be undertaking Modern Slavery practices, this increased to 15 percent in Tier 2 and 35 percent amongst Tier 3 suppliers. Almost three quarters of respondents believed that some modern slavery existed at the Tier 3 level (Lake et al, 2015).

The more vertical integration that a global company has, the less likely that worker abuse will occur. However, this of course can be a more expensive option in terms of supply chain costs – although this is not necessarily the case if reputational damage (and other risks) are factored in. In fact, the impact of a disaster, such as the Rana Plaza factory collapse in 2011, upon a brand is now recognized as being a major driver of change. The Ethical Trade Initiative report on Modern Slavery asserted, 'Most companies [in the study] felt that mitigating risks to workers [in their supply chains] was ultimately mitigating risk to the business' (Lake et al 2015).

These days, few global brands own their own supply chains. Virtual networks are the norm with thousands of suppliers being used, especially in sectors where the goods are largely commoditized (such as fashion and textiles). One of the strategies being employed to create more visibility is to consolidate purchases around a smaller number of suppliers. Not only does this mean more buying power, but there is also more leverage to implement sustainable and ethical practices. This not only extends to Tier 1 but also (in theory) to Tier 2 and Tier 3 suppliers. This could be referred to as a more activist approach which can deliver all-round benefits. One of the downsides with consolidating production in a smaller number of locations, however, is that disruption from events such as natural disasters, fires or industrial action is greater. A balance needs to be struck between the commercial needs of the company and a range of supply chain threats as well as sustainable and ethical considerations.

Ethical initiatives which involve the collaboration of multiple Western manufacturers or retailers have been shown to be very effective. One of the problems which many companies have faced when trying to create change related to working conditions is their lack of leverage higher up the supply chain. Even very large international buyers may only represent a small proportion of a supplier's output and therefore exerting enough pressure relies on a significant number of buyers grouping together to insist on improvements in employee conditions. This problem is possibly getting worse rather than better. For example, when sourcing goods from China, international buyers are dwarfed in importance by local retailers and manufacturers which may have far fewer scruples in terms of ethical behaviour (in fact this applies to environmental practices as well as labour). The example of the Uyghur community is a case in point dealt with later in this chapter. Getting suppliers to improve their behaviour towards employees is consequently far harder. There is often the issue, as well, that many Western buyers are much smaller in size than the suppliers that they are buying from, and consequently have little or no leverage over their behaviour.

Attitudes to competition and specifically competition law may also stand in the way of effective cooperative efforts to develop ethical supply chains. Many companies are unwilling to talk to their rivals, either because their supply chain is seen as a competitive advantage and there is no desire to share information or because they are fearful that competition regulators may take action against them. This has led to independent, third-party organizations being established to ensure that communication can exist between companies in a certain market within the bounds of legislation. NGOs can play a role in this, such as the 'Stronger Together' initiative, a multi-stakeholder business-led initiative aiming to reduce modern slavery.

MODERN SLAVERY LEGISLATION

Several international and national organizations and governments have published guidelines and legislation which companies sourcing goods from around the world are either encouraged or compelled to comply with:

- UN Guiding Principles on Business and Human Rights
- California Transparency in Supply Chains Act
- European Convention on Human Rights
- European Union Directive (2014/95/EU)
- UK Modern Slavery Act, 2015
- OECD Guidelines for Multinational Enterprises

According to the International Labour Organization (ILO) there are 21 million people in forced labour throughout the world – some of whom inevitably will be working in supply chains which reach into developed markets (ILO, 2021). Most of those in slavery are based in Asia, although the issue also exists in developed countries, such as the UK, where it is estimated 10–12,000 people could be considered in slavery. In fact, the survey undertaken by the Ethical Trade Initiative found that 71 percent of companies believed that there was a likelihood of modern slavery occurring in their supply chains.

Table 12.1 Forced labour worldwide

Region	No of people subject to modern slavery
Asia	11,700,000
Africa	3,700,000
Middle East	600,000
Latin America	1,800,000
CIS, Central and Southeast Europe	1,600,000
Europe/North America	1,500,000

Source: International Labour Organization 2021

A report by the lobby organization, KnowTheChain, estimated that forced labour generates $150 billion in illegal profits each year (KTC, 2016).

In 2015 the UK government passed the Modern Slavery Act which sought to address the problem of 'slavery, servitude and forced or compulsory labour' in the global supply chains of UK companies. It placed a responsibility on companies over a certain threshold in size (£36 million in turnover) to publish a statement on their slavery and human trafficking policies and what they were doing to ensure that modern slavery was not occurring in their supply chains. As Theresa May, the Home Secretary at the time, commented,

> It is simply not acceptable for any organization to say, in the twenty-first century, that they did not know [about modern slavery in their supply chains]. It is not acceptable for organizations to ignore the issue because it is difficult or complex. And, it is certainly not acceptable for organizations to put profit above the welfare and wellbeing of its employees and those working on its behalf.
>
> *(Home Office, 2015).*

Guidance related to the Act advises that companies should undertake an audit of their suppliers to ensure that they do not undertake unethical practices. It then sets out procedures for how companies should deal with issues which are uncovered, which includes contacting local NGOs, trade unions or the national government. Although there are no mechanisms for forcing UK companies to stop buying goods or services from a supplier which does not comply, the government clearly believes that they will feel pressurized by the unwelcome publicity which would otherwise be generated.

The UK government is quick to point out that there are benefits to companies which will accrue from compliance with the new law:

These include:

1. protecting and enhancing an organization's reputation and brand
2. protecting and growing the organization's customer base as more consumers seek out businesses with higher ethical standards
3. improved investor confidence
4. greater staff retention and loyalty based on values and respect and
5. developing more responsive, stable and innovative supply chains.

One of the problems related to the legislation is the difficulty in identifying when 'modern slavery' is actually taking place. As the government itself admits, there is a spectrum of abuse and poor labour conditions and practices do not themselves constitute a contravention of the law unless a level of coercion exists. Regulations themselves are not enough to ensure employee protection in global supply chains – companies still retain a moral as well as regulatory responsibility for their suppliers' practices.

THE ETHICS OF SOURCING FROM CHINA

Controversy over the sourcing of materials and manufactured goods from the Xinjiang Uyghur Autonomous Region (XUAR) of China is just the latest in a long list of ethical and environmental scandals related to supply chains originating in the country.

A coalition of human rights groups has accused the Chinese authorities of a state-sponsored system of detention and forced labour affecting up to 1.8 million Uyghur and other Muslim people. It has been estimated that a fifth of all cotton products manufactured in the world is in some way connected to the region, potentially implicating many global brands (Coalition to End Uyghur Forced Labour, 2021). The automotive sector is also affected. One report states that Western manufacturers are unwittingly sourcing steel and aluminium, tyres, brakes, windscreens and batteries from the region (Murphy et al, 2022).

The widespread condemnation of the practices allegedly being employed in the XUAR has led many manufacturers and retailers to urgently undertake audits of their supply chains. Where evidence has been found of even indirect supply of materials, some companies, H&M being the most widely reported, have severed links. However, although this has gone some way towards appeasing many lobbyists, it has meant that the Western companies involved have fallen foul of the Chinese authorities which have consequently orchestrated a political campaign against them. This has resulted in Chinese e-commerce companies, including Alibaba and JD.com, removing some international labels from their platforms; Chinese celebrities denouncing the brands which they had previously worked for and walkouts staged by Chinese workers from the stores of their employers. Other brands affected were Adidas, Nike, Burberry and Gap, all of which condemned the practice of forced labour.

Nike's response is fairly typical of many other Western manufacturers. In a statement, the company said,

> Nike is committed to ethical and responsible manufacturing and we uphold international labor standards. We are concerned about reports of forced labor in, and connected to, the Xinjiang Uyghur Autonomous Region (XUAR)... Nike takes very seriously any reports about forced labor and we have been engaging with multi-stakeholder working groups to assess collective solutions that will help preserve the integrity of our global supply chains.
>
> *(Nike, 2021)*

However, not all manufacturers and retailers have followed suit. According to the *New York Times*, some companies have continued to source from the region, mindful of the huge market or just unaware that many of the goods in their supply chains originate in the XUAR. This is despite recent legislation in the US and other countries outlawing the importation of goods from the region (Swanson, 2022). Inevitably, Chinese brands will be the biggest winners from shutting out Western rivals, willingly supporting the Chinese government line.

The issue raises a number of important points for international manufacturers and retailers.

First, it is critical to ensure that they have complete visibility of their supply chains, even down to raw material level. This is possible, but only at a cost.

Second, the decision to source from alternative regions and suppliers ('China Plus' strategies) will also increase costs, but this is essential unless the company wants to tarnish its brand or lose sales in Western markets.

Third, Western lobbyists, investors and consumers have demonstrated that they have the power to influence sourcing decisions and this is likely to become an important factor in the development of supply chains in the future, especially in emerging markets.

Fourth, China's policy of encouraging anti-global brand sentiment (Standaert, 2021) may eventually force Western companies into making a binary choice. They won't be allowed to continue serving the huge Chinese market whilst boycotting a certain region or criticizing certain policies. This is a sign of confidence by the Chinese government and a thorny problem for international companies. Ignoring the Chinese market is not an option for many due to its size and growth, as well as the fact that the value of their share price is to an extent predicated on the access to this lucrative market. If they are forced out of the market then, as has been seen in the Uyghur example, Chinese rivals with their nascent brands will move in. However, if global manufacturers and retailers continue to source from China, accepting (or at least turning a blind eye to) ethical and environmental issues, they will face sustained criticism from Western consumers, lobbyists and ethical investors as well as legal action by governments.

In effect, the Chinese government response to the Uyghur controversy is a statement of intent which could lead to a *de facto* 'Sinification' of some supply chains. It is another sign of the potential bifurcation of global supply chains, a process already underway in high-tech sectors where Western governments are eliminating the use of Chinese components in infrastructure such as that related to the 5G rollout for security reasons (see Chapter 5).

In the case of the Uyghurs, however, the separation of supply chains is being driven as much by the Chinese government as the West. The inevitable result will be the same: one set of supply chains serving the West and another, with a different values and priorities, serving China's sphere of interest in Asia and the countries in its Belt and Road Initiative.

The politicization of supply chains caused by the treatment of the Uyghurs by the Chinese government has set an important precedent. There are many issues which could well have bigger ramifications, such as human rights violations in Hong Kong or even China's relationship with Taiwan. Likewise, companies may even be required by shareholders and investors to make a stand on environmental matters such as China's program of constructing coal-fired power stations. Strengthening sentiment on both sides is leading to a transformation in supply chain architecture which will have inevitable cost implications for businesses and consumers.

CONCLUSION

An ethical approach to global sourcing is fundamental to the future supply chain management strategies of global manufacturers and retailers. However, whilst it is easy to publish statements of intent, the reality of implementing an ethical policy involves cost implications, management time, focus and resources as well as often requiring awkward decisions. These costs will be offset in the longer term by ensuring that operations and brand become more resilient, although the benefits may not be immediately obvious.

There may also be continued opposition to what could be seen as the imposition of Western ethics on cultures and economies which work to a different set of practices and values. China does not accept the West's accusations of human rights violations regarding the way it has treated the Uyghur community and asserts that opposition from Western governments and companies has been politically motivated.

The progress that has been made over recent years in improving the conditions of workers in global supply chains should not be under-estimated. Indeed, this has brought about important societal benefits in developing countries. There may be limits, however, on the pressure which Western lobbyists, businesses and governments can exert before the pressure becomes regarded as undue and unwelcome political interference. If this is the case, then ultimately there is a risk that the blurring of ethical policies with international politics could result in the splintering of established global supply chain structures. This, in economic terms at least, would mean the development of sub-optimal distribution channels; costly to build and maintain. Whether the outcome would be positive for workers, consumers or for international relations will depend to a large degree on perspective.

REFERENCES

Coalition to End Uyghur Forced Labour (2021) Open Letter to UN High Commissioner for Human Rights: Coalition Calls for Public Reporting on Uyghur Forced Labour, Coalition to End Uyghur Forced Labour. Available from https://enduyghurforcedlabour.org /open-letter-to-un-high-commissioner-for-human-rights-coalition -calls-for-public-reporting-on-uyghur-forced-labour/

Home Office (2015) Transparency in Supply Chains: A Practical Guide, Home Office, UK.

ILO (2021) 21 million people are now victims of forced labour, ILO says, International Labour Organization. Available at http://www .ilo.org/global/about-the-ilo/newsroom/news/WCMS_181961/ lang--en/index.htm

KTC (2016) ICT Benchmark Findings Report, KnowTheChain, UK.

Lake, Q, MacAlister, J et al (2015) Corporate approaches to addressing modern slavery in supply chains: a snapshot of current practice, Ethical Trade Initiative, UK.

Murphy, L, Salcito, K, Uluyol, Y and Rabkin, M (2022) Driving Force: Automotive Supply Chains and Forced Labor in the Uyghur Region, Sheffield Hallam University. Available from www.shu .ac.uk/helena-kennedy-centre-international-justice/research-and -projects/all-projects/driving-force

Nike (2021) XUAR Statement, Nike. Available from https:// admin.about.nike.com/media/files/949e2527-4f64-4a37-af44 -8467064deb8f/XUAR-Statement.pdf

Standaert, M (2021) Nike and H&M face backlash in China over Xinjiang statements, The Guardian. Available from www. theguardian.com/world/2021/mar/25/nike-and-hm-face-backlash -in-china-over-xinjiang-statements

Swanson, A (2022) Companies brace for impact of new forced labor law, New York Times. Available from www.nytimes.com/2022 /06/22/us/politics/xinjiang-uyghur-forced- labor-law.html

13

The Supply Chain Costs of 'Digital Decoupling'

INTRODUCTION

The impact of data protection legislation on the flow of supply chain data is often overlooked when examining headwinds to globalization. Whilst China has become the focus of controversy over its attempts to 'digitally decouple' from the rest of the world, the EU and US have also developed their own regulatory environments which threaten to slow or prevent the transfer of cross-border data between supply chain parties.

For example, the access which China's government demands to company data means that the export of certain types of data generated in Europe and US is now prohibited, although this was not always the case. In the past, data transfers between China and the rest of the world were asymmetric; that is, it was easier for a Chinese company to export data from other countries back to China than the reverse. This is now starting to change. The tightening of Europe's General Data Protection Regulation (GDPR) has meant that data can only be transferred to a jurisdiction which has a similar level of data protection to that in the European Economic Area.

Similarly, the Chinese government also controls exports of data, although its policy is driven by the belief that much of the data generated by companies and consumers within its borders should be treated as a strategic resource, rather than from any concerns over privacy.

As this chapter will demonstrate, the last five years has seen a mass of barrier-building legislation, leading to significant restrictions on data flows. Moreover, whilst many of the problems facing globalization apply to specific industry verticals (e.g. pharmaceuticals or semiconductors), the barriers being built to restrict movements of data apply to all sectors and can be particularly damaging. As an increasing number of countries develop their own data laws, there is the risk of even more fragmentation.

INCOMPATIBLE DATA REGIMES

The lack of compatibility between the way in which authorities define and manage data is an obvious challenge for companies seeking to comply with the requirements of various regulatory regimes. Each market requires a different data strategy, compliance officers and even technology to ensure that rules are being observed. Failure to do so can be punished severely in financial terms.

This 'patchwork globalization', as it has been termed, means that businesses are unable to pool their worldwide data resources. To illustrate this point, if a consumer goods manufacturer had operations in the US, EU and China it should, in theory, have access to information on the behaviour of 2.2 billion potential customers. Data localization policies mean that, in reality, companies have access to three pools of data: 1.4 billion consumers in China; 450 million in the EU and 330 million in the US. For some companies this is less of a problem. Many consumer goods or automotive manufacturers which are operationally embedded in one or each of these markets will be able to use these discrete data pools to effectively customize products to local tastes. However, global companies which seek to distribute products on a worldwide basis will be disadvantaged by the quality and quantity of data which they are able to transfer to their corporate head office.

THE DEVELOPMENT OF DATA 'ISLANDS'

From a purely commercial perspective it would be in the interests of businesses if regulators of all the major markets were able to align data standards and take a similar position on issues such as privacy. In reality, this is unlikely due to the strategic importance which many governments place on data, especially relating to national security.

As part of its programme to facilitate the growth of cross-border e-commerce, the World Trade Organization (WTO) is seeking to drive data regulation harmonization – a critical step towards providing open markets, not least for developing countries. The WTO's stance is that, '...cross-border data flows support digital inclusion, as witnessed during the Covid-19 pandemic, where entrepreneurs, start-ups and small businesses were enabled to participate in the global digital economy more efficiently' (WTO, 2021). It is the organization's view that in many cases data localization policies are largely value destructive as they can deny customers access to global technologies without delivering benefits of security, protection or easier access to data by law enforcement agencies. Furthermore, the creation of multiple 'data stacks' through forced localization requirements provides a competitive advantage for 'national heroes', or at least those companies with large local market share, and disadvantages foreign market entrants. This in turn hurts local consumers through higher prices and businesses through the lack of access to technology and innovation.

However, despite the WTO's argument, much of the world seems committed to the creation of discrete data 'islands' which will compromise supply chains and harm economic development. Set out below are the policies being actively pursued by China, the EU and the US. These are not only important in their own right as the world's largest traders, but also because they will be used as models for other countries. More authoritarian governments will inevitably look to China's lead whilst others in the democratic West are more likely to adopt the practices of either the EU or US.

CHINA'S 'TECHNO-NATIONALISM'

China's data laws

China passed two laws in 2021 with implications for global supply chains: the Data Security Law (DSL) and the Personal Information Protection Law (PIPL). In substance, the legislation mirrors the EU's General Data Protection Regulation (GDPR) although in China the state has far more control over the system in contrast to independent arbitrators in Europe. Some aspects of the legislation are liberalizing, designed to make government data available to companies in order to boost economic growth through innovation. However, there are also purely political elements of the law which make it possible for the Chinese government to retaliate against countries which it believes have adopted discriminatory measures (namely, the US).

A report undertaken by the Mercator Institute and European Union Chamber of Commerce in China (EUCCC) (EUCCC, 2021) warns that, as a result, global businesses face the choice of two data strategies driven by the challenges of coping with issues such as national security, individual privacy rights, technology standards, licensing requirements and of course economic concerns.

1. Establish two separate digital stacks: one for China and one for the rest of the world. The first approach would require partnering or outsourcing to local Chinese companies.
2. Build a 'flexible architecture', founded on neutral technologies which can use modular components able to be swapped in and out depending on local regulations.

Either way, this exercise of 'techno-nationalism', as the authors of the report call it, will be costly in terms of its impact on innovation, efficiency and economies of scale. It may even result in companies pulling out of the market if it is marginal in terms of business importance.

There will also be unintended consequences. When introduced, the laws had an immediate impact on transportation systems, not because they were specifically included within the legislation but due to confusion over how these laws would be interpreted and enforced. The penalties for breaching the new regulations are so high that companies have erred on the side of caution as highlighted in the case study below.

NEW DATA LAWS DISRUPT VESSEL LOCATION TOOLS

The ability to track cargo ships has become an essential element of many supply chain visibility tools, helping shippers and other partners to identify the location of shipments and their estimated time of arrival at their destination port. One of the most important of these tracking tools is Automatic Identification System (AIS), which relies on satellite technology, coastal networks and vessel transmission to inform users of vessel location. This information is also critical in preventing vessel collisions, organizing port logistics, congestion analysis and route planning as well as ensuring compliance with economic sanctions.

In November 2021, following the adoption of the PIPL and DSL, Chinese providers dramatically cut the amount of data being exported due to fears that they might be transgressing the new laws. According to one source, the number of vessels in Chinese waters which could be tracked fell from 100,000 a day on 28 October to just 15,000 on 17 November. At the time, the head trade analyst of VesselsValue commented, 'Terrestrial AIS signals typically provide the greatest data coverage and insight into shipping in Chinese ports, so this data decline could significantly impact ocean supply chain visibility across

China, one of the world's major importers of coal and iron ore and exporters of containers'. (Whelan, 2021).

Although the outage lasted only a few weeks, the episode reveals the level of disruption to logistics systems which can be caused from data regulations. Supply chain managers should be aware of these types of threats to data flows, given the political nature of the Chinese data laws and their provisions for retaliatory measures against the West.

Telecoms services constrained

The Chinese government's policy related to foreign investment by telecommunications companies is also highly restrictive. In many cases, a 50:50 joint venture is required which is often (although not always) an insurmountable barrier to market access. This not only means that foreign companies are missing out on a large and growing market through their inability to offer, for example, cloud services, but also the opportunity to provide fourth industrial revolution technologies such as internet of things (IoT). As the EUCCC says, 'The playing field in the digital arena in China is largely set up to prevent foreign participation on an equal footing. The market remains only partially open, and the conditions for entry are very demanding even when options seemingly exist' (EUCCC, 2021). This is not only damaging to the foreign company, but also to the Chinese economy which loses out on the transfer of technological knowledge. This often means that global companies managing supply chains in the market cannot access the same quality of services which are present elsewhere in the world.

Projecting China's data framework globally

Notwithstanding the barriers which it has erected to hinder the export of data from its own shores, the Chinese government has been vociferous in the defence of the free flow of global supply chain data throughout the rest of the world.

First set out in September 2020, China's Global Data Security Initiative (GDSI) was established in response to President Trump's allegations that China was untrustworthy partner as regards to data security. The first of its avowed aims is to create a global framework for dealing with data and digital commerce to, '...maintain open, secure and stable supply chains' (Park, 2022). To achieve this China believes that a multilateral approach is necessary and since its launch China's government has gained support from a number of other countries involved with the Belt and Road Initiative, such as Russia and the Arab League. 'China has put forward the initiative with the aim of safeguarding global data and supply chain security, promoting development of the digital economy, and providing a basis for international rules-making in this area', foreign ministry spokesperson, Zhao Lijian is quoted as saying (Tiezzi, 2020). China's Foreign Minister, Wang Yi also commented, 'Protectionism in the digital domain runs counter to the laws of economic development and the trend of globalization. Protectionist practices undermine the right of global consumers to equally access digital services and will eventually hold back the country's own development' (Guan, 2020).

Despite these claims that the GDSI has been developed to negotiate a multilateral framework which will underpin the importance of data to global supply chains, in reality the initiative is actually a backdoor to data localization. The Chinese government has pushed for years to ensure that data which is generated locally is held locally, as it believes this provides for greater levels of control over its people and the businesses operating within its borders. If GDSI were indeed agreed on a multilateral basis (which is unlikely) this policy would consolidate the existing barriers to data flows. At the same time as this, China wants to ensure that it is not cut off from flows of data which will be critical to the growth of its economy by positioning its own data regulations as equivalent to other major jurisdictions.

EUROPEAN UNION'S 'GOLD STANDARD'

The EU's approach to data protection and privacy is regarded globally as a 'gold standard' and as such it has been widely copied, even by China. Its most far-reaching legislation, the General Data Protection Regulation (GDPR), came into force across Europe in 2018.

In terms of global supply chains, GDPR has an extraterritorial impact which was highlighted by the so-called 'Schrems II' ruling by the European Court of Justice which directed that data could only be transferred from the EU to jurisdictions which offer similar levels of data protection. This ruling has had an impact on the ability of companies to export data not only to China, but also to the US, as will be discussed. After Brexit, many of its provisions were enshrined into a UK law which is regarded as 'essentially equivalent' by the European Commission; hence data can flow freely between the two jurisdictions.

A more recent EU law, the Data Governance Act, defers in the main to existing GDPR legislation but it also strengthens controls over the transfer of EU data to third countries from public-sector bodies in instances where intellectual property or trade secrets are involved.

The EU has also passed legislation which will affect how the major platforms (e.g. online search engines, video-sharing services, web browsers etc) control content and use and protect the data which they generate (the 'Digital Services Act' (DSA) and 'Digital Markets Act' (DMA)). This will increase levels of regulatory compliance and influence the way in which platforms will be required to interact with governments, customers and competitors. The main targets of the new regulations are companies such as Google, Amazon, Apple, Meta and Microsoft. Indeed, Apple has criticized the DMA, saying its provisions will, '...create unnecessary privacy and security vulnerabilities for our users, while others will prohibit us from charging for the intellectual property in which we invest heavily' (Chang, 2022).

Furthermore, a new Data Act is presently being discussed, addressing who can use and access data generated in the EU. The law is designed to develop a framework for a 'big data' environment created by Fourth Industrial Revolution innovations such as internet of things. According to a European Commission press release, 'The volume of data is constantly growing, from 33 zettabytes generated in 2018 to 175 zettabytes expected in 2025. It is an untapped potential, 80% of industrial data is never used. The Data Act addresses the legal, economic and technical issues that lead to data being under-used' (EC, 2022). The Act will have supply chain benefits in as much as the legislation will facilitate better access to databases for all parties, allowing, for instance, after market service providers to develop and compete with original equipment manufacturers.

The rulings and legislation in Europe over the past five years have been designed to integrate a previously fragmented environment; lay the foundations for dealing with 'big data' needs as well as exert more control over the global tech giants. At the same time as facilitating easier movement of data within the EU, the legislation also makes it more difficult for companies to transfer data out of the region. Although there are good reasons for this – it is hard to argue against putting safeguards in place which regulate the movement of sensitive, commercial or personal data – the fact remains that they place an additional burden on companies trying to do business on a global scale.

USA PLAYS CATCH-UP

The USA has struggled for years to pass a federal law which would protect its citizens' data privacy. This state of affairs is now being addressed as a matter of urgency. In 2019 the National Security and Personal Data Act was developed under the Trump regime to counter what has been seen by many as, '...Beijing's declared strategic ambitions, its ongoing campaigns of global cyberespionage, and weak legal constraints on the Chinese Communist Party's coercive power over domestic technology companies.' (Williams, 2020). The bill would have prohibited the transfer of data to, and storage of data within, foreign countries that are deemed to threaten US national security. Although this law was not passed, a successor bill, the American Data Privacy and Protection Act (ADPPA), is expected to pass into law due to bipartisan support.

ADPPA will provide a national framework to protect consumers' data on a domestic and, crucially, cross-border basis. It restricts the transfer of data to specific countries including China, Russia, Iran and North Korea. Despite this, as one law company comments, '...the ADPPA does not contain provisions with teeth relating to data localisation and cross-border data restrictions. The practical impact of this part of the bill for multinationals and supply chains beginning in mainland China is still to be seen' (Roberts and Ke, 2022).

Although China is the main focus of the US government's data policy, it will also address challenging relations with the European Union. It would be easy to assume that the two jurisdictions would be allies against more authoritarian regimes and this looked to be the case when the EU–US Privacy Shield was formed in 2017. The 'Shield' was designed to, '...provide companies on both sides of the Atlantic with a mechanism to comply with data protection requirements when transferring personal data from the European Union and Switzerland to the United States in support of transatlantic commerce' (ITA, 2022). However, the Schrems II ruling (see above) held that the US was not equivalent to the EU in terms of its safeguards of data security. This put the initiative on hold until late 2022, when, after work by US authorities strengthening safeguards for signals intelligence activities, to developing a new redress mechanism and updating privacy principles for US organizations, the European Commission published a positive 'adequacy' decision. The new EU–US Data Privacy Framework will now be reviewed by the European Parliament and Member States. The White House commented, 'By advancing cross-border data flows, the new framework will promote an inclusive digital economy in which all people can participate and in which companies of all sizes from all of our countries can thrive' (White House, 2022). Important as the agreement is in its own right, it may also prove useful as a foundation for further trade data agreements with Mexico, Canada and Japan. This 'plurilateral' approach contrasts with China's attempt to develop a multilateral agreement and even with earlier attempts by President Trump to unilaterally isolate China.

CONCLUSION

Despite the tensions which have developed between the US, Europe and China over the last decade, a complete disruption to data flows is unlikely, unless of course there is a major geopolitical crisis, such as the invasion of Taiwan. More probable is a gradual evolution of data relations over the coming years, sometimes becoming more restrictive, at others more liberalized, depending on the prevailing political situation. This will still mean, however, that present engrained inefficiencies continue to exist in the way that data is handled, adding costs and stifling innovation especially in addressing global problems such as climate change.

REFERENCES

Chang, N (2022) EU's Digital Markets Act comes into force: what is it, and what does it mean for big tech? Euronews. Available from https://www.euronews.com/next/2022/ 11/02/eus-digital-markets -act-comes-into-force-what-is-it-and-what-does-it-mean-for- big -tech

Congress (2019) National Security and Personal Data Protection Act of 2019, US Congress. Available from www.congress.gov/bill /116th-congress/senate-bill/2889

EC (2022) Data Act: Commission proposes measures for a fair and innovative data economy, European Commission. Available from https://ec.europa.eu/commission/presscorner/detail/en/ip_22 _1113

EUCCC (2021) Decoupling: Severed Ties and Patchwork Globalisation, European Union Chamber of Commerce in China. Available from https://merics.org/sites/default/files/ 2021-01/ Decoupling_EN.pdf

Guan, L (2020) Chinese Government pursues global data security initiatives, CIOTech Asia. Available from https://ciotechasia.com/ chinese-government-pursues-global-data- security-initiatives/

ITA (2022) Privacy Shield program overview, International Trade Administration. Available from https://www.privacyshield.gov/

Park, C (2022) Knowledge Base: China's 'Global Data Security Initiative', Stanford University. Available from https://digichina .stanford.edu/work/knowledge-base- chinas-global-data-security -initiative/

Roberts, A and Ke, T (2022) China in the spotlight: US federal data and privacy bill unveiled, Linklaters. Available from https:// techinsights.linklaters.com/post/102hqbv/ china-in-the-spotlight -us-federal-data-and-privacy-bill-unveiled

Tiezzi, S (2020) China's bid to write the global rules on data security, The Diplomat. Available from https://thediplomat.com/2020/09/ chinas-bid-to-write-the-global-rules- on-data-security/

Whelan, S (2021) New law in China coincides with massive cut in vessel location data, The Loadstar. Available from https:// theloadstar.com/new-law-in-china-coincides- with-massive-cut -in-vessel-location-data/

White House (2022) United States and European Commission Joint Statement on Trans-Atlantic Data Privacy Framework, White House, Washington, DC.

Williams, R (2020) To enhance data security, federal privacy legislation is just a start, Brookings Institute. Available from www .brookings.edu/techstream/to-enhance-data-   security-federal -privacy-legislation-is-just-a-start/

WTO (2021) E-commerce negotiations advance, delve deeper into data issues, World Trade Organisation. Available from www.wto .org/english/news_e/news21_e/jsec_ 20may21_e.htm

14

Conclusion

THE WORLD 'UNFLATTENED'

Although it is too early to call time on the globalized 'flat world' described in Thomas Friedman's book of 2005, there is no doubt that major changes to global supply chains are underway and have been since the high watermark reached just before the Great Recession of 2008/9. Increasing geo-political tensions, exacerbated by the rise of China, domestic disillusionment and the Covid-19 pandemic, are leading to the fragmentation of international trade and a weakening of institutions, such as the WTO, as changing political, economic and security priorities unravel 75 years of liberalization.

In fact, Friedman himself recognized that the world was never entirely 'flat' – rather it was in the process of being 'flattened'. In his words, 'It is not historically inevitable that the rest of the world will become flat or that already flat parts of the world won't get unflattened by war, economic disruption or politics' (Friedman, 2005). Since he wrote the book, economic and political 'seismic forces' have made the landscape far more mountainous than he might have envisaged.

GLOBALIZATION CANCELLED

This is a challenging time for the globalized system of trading upon which most of the prosperity of the last few decades has been founded. Only recently have Western politicians recognized that China has been allowed to use supply chains and international transport networks as a route to project its power globally. Formerly, most opposition to globalization came from the labour organizations which have seen many of their members made unemployed due to what they regard as unfair and foreign state subsidized competition (and in many cases they have been proved right). Many manufacturers and suppliers in the US steel industry, for example, complain that they have been forced to shutter operations due to the costs of environmental regulations to which competitors in many foreign countries do not have to adhere.

For decades we have seen the rolling back of protectionism, where the influence of domestic and international politics waned as a consideration in global trade relations. Economic imperatives achieved primacy due to the belief that the value which was created by trade liberalisation benefited all parties. Unfortunately, not all this value was shared and many parts of society in the West lost out. On top of this, it could be argued that not enough value was shared with labour in Asia (and other low-cost manufacturing locations) to placate those who believed that globalization's benefits were predicated on the exploitation of foreign workers.

Beyond this, Western politicians have finally woken up to the threat to security presented by the outsourcing of strategic elements of manufacturing to third countries. However, the decades' long development of highly complex production supply chain networks and ecosystems cannot be unravelled quickly without inflicting huge damage on the global economy, especially in sectors such as high-tech, automotive, chemicals, pharmaceuticals and aerospace. China and the West will be aware of the limitations of their rhetoric in the face of economic realities.

Regulation of global supply chains is now also being used to engineer environmental and societal outcomes by trading access to Western domestic markets in return for commitment to more sustainable policies and behaviour. Whilst this may seem a perfectly reasonable exchange, it may also be seen by many in developing countries as a form of Western power projection, even 'neo-colonialism'.

NOT DEAD YET

Although it would be convenient to pronounce the end of global supply chains, that is not the aim of this book and nor do I believe that to be the case. Rather, although globalization was once the dominant economic orthodoxy to which all others were subordinated, it is now just one of many. This means an increased level of supply chain complexity and higher costs which ultimately will have to be paid for by consumers and taxpayers. However, the benefits of globalization have only ever been narrowly defined and the societal, environmental, ethical, security and political costs conveniently ignored. Whether a new paradigm of fragmentation, localization and protectionism does a better job at addressing these policy challenges is yet to be seen.

Having said that, it will take many years to unravel the structures which have built up in the last few decades and which have become deeply engrained economically. In a number of sectors, such as semiconductor manufacturing, some countries' comparative advantages are so great that building an alternative model may be impossible, despite politicians' aspirations.

In my opinion, reshoring, near-sourcing and optionalized sourcing strategies ('China plus') will gather momentum in strategic industry sectors as the world bifurcates between the West and China. This trend will be reinforced by volatile oil and gas prices and the imposition of carbon taxes which will provide an advantage to countries with access to reliable, low-cost energy resources. It will also make regionalized distribution models which are dependent on long distance and/or international transport less attractive to shippers.

The free market philosophy which underpinned globalization was never wrong in itself. However, all markets need rules and when the rules of the liberalized trading regime were not properly enforced, some countries – most significantly China – were able to subvert the system into which they had been admitted. For most countries and institutions, China is now too big to challenge politically or economically and has achieved a position of such importance in the developed and developing world that even Germany will not contemplate 'decoupling' due to the financial ramifications. This has left other countries, led by the USA, with few options but to withdraw from this Chinese version of globalization, build alternative or retreat behind protectionist barriers. To use the phrase introduced in the preface, 'It wasn't meant to be this way...'.

REFERENCE

Friedman, T (2005) The World is Flat, Penguin, London.

Acknowledgements

I would like to extend my gratitude to all my colleagues in the supply chain industry whose knowledge and help have made this book possible. In particular, I would like to thank Sarah Smith, Ken Lyon and all the team at Transport Intelligence for their on-going support and insight. I would also like to thank my long-term publisher, Julia Swales, who has been so encouraging over the past decade and I am delighted that *The Death of Globalization* is the first fruit of her new publishing venture.

I would like to dedicate this book to my wife, Sara, who has been tireless in her support over the past 25 years, all the while accomplishing great things in her own profession and bringing up our two sons.